Unforgettable EMMAUS

A Celebration

PUBLICATIONS COMMITTEE: Roger Whitcomb, Corrine Durdock, Craig Neely,
C. Richard Chartrand, Marge Heatley, Johanna Green, and Teri Sorg-McManamon

PHOTO CREDITS: C. Richard Chartrand, Jane Deutsch, Emmaus Historical Society,
Emmaus Public Library, Teri Madison, and Bob Boehmer

BOOK DESIGN: Susan Eugster
PRODUCTION: TN Printing

The information on the businesses, organizations, and churches
listed in this commemorative book are the result of responses received
from our requests for information. Although we realize there are many
more entities that could have been listed, we could only list the
ones who responded to our requests.

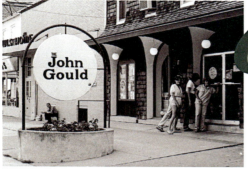

Contents

PROCLAMATION 2008 - 230

BOROUGH OF EMMAUS
150 YEAR ANNIVERSARY CELEBRATION
AND
250TH YEAR AS A MORAVIAN COMMUNITY

WHEREAS, on behalf of Borough officials, I extend a hearty and sincere welcome to former residents, friends, neighboring communities, and out of state guests; and

WHEREAS, the official celebration of the One Hundred Fifty Year Anniversary of the Borough will begin **January, 2009** and end **December, 2009**; and

WHEREAS, the Borough of Emmaus will celebrate its 250th year as a Moravian Community; and

WHEREAS, this great celebration will showcase Emmaus throughout Pennsylvania; and

WHEREAS, this **150 Year Anniversary** would not have been done without the dedication of the Anniversary Committee who worked many hours; and

WHEREAS, we say thank you to everyone who contributed in one way or another.

AND, NOW THEREFORE, I Winfield Iobst, Mayor of the Borough of Emmaus, and on behalf of Borough Council wish everyone a Prosperous 2009 and again welcome you to come to Emmaus and enjoy the events that will be held throughout the year.

DONE this 15th day of December in the year Two Thousand Eight in the Borough of Emmaus, Lehigh County, Pennsylvania.

BOROUGH OF EMMAUS

MAYOR WINFIELD IOBST

EMMAUS BOROUGH COUNCIL
Left to Right: Brent Labenberg, Brian Holtzhafer,
Wesley R. Barrett, Dr. Michael Waddell,
Mayor Winfield Iobst, Craig Neely,
Lee Ann Gilbert, and Nathan Brown

Mayor's Letter

IT HAS BEEN QUITE AN HONOR for me to serve you as mayor of Emmaus during our 2009 Anniversary Celebration—a dual anniversary celebrating 150 years as a borough and 250 years as a community. Who would have thought that in 1959 my father, Theodore W. Iobst, as the mayor of Emmaus, would take part in the burying of the 1959 Time Capsule, and now I, as mayor fifty years later, have the privilege and honor of taking part in the burying of the 2009 Time Capsule. What a wonderful year of events this has been! Many events were held leading up to the "Big Weekend": The dedication of the new Triangle Park, the Anniversary Parade (which included performances by the reunited Emmaus Sentinels Drum and Bugle Corps), festivities at Community Park, the opening of the 1959 Time Capsule, and the unprecedented and spectacular Fireworks display at Emmaus High School! The events continued with the Wildlife Art Show, the Weekend Train Excursions, and a PA Dutch Play, to name a few. It was a successful year, but success was due to all of the planning and the hard work of the hundreds of volunteers. My thanks and appreciation go out to the Anniversary Committee, the Project Teams, and all of the Emmaus Community Service Groups/Organizations. I wish to extend a special thank-you to our Borough Police, Fire, Ambulance, and Public Works Departments. They kept us safe and secure. The collaboration and teamwork of all of these groups gave our residents and visitors a year to remember. We can truly say "Unforgettable Emmaus."

{ 1

GOD BLESS,

Mayor W. Iobst

EMMAUS MY HOME

"I love to live in Emmaus where the trees meet across the street,
Where you wave your hand and say 'hello' to everyone you meet;
I like to visit the stores in town where you can hear the gossip that goes around.
Our life is interwoven with the people we learn to know,
And we share with their joys and sorrows as they come and go;
I love Emmaus, it's my hometown, and I care no more to roam,
For every house in Emmaus is more than a house, it's a home."

— WINFIELD IOBST

Emmaus
2009
Anniversary

Introduction

THIS PUBLICATION WAS CONCEIVED as a method of conveying to the public and preserving for posterity the events and activities of Emmaus's 250/150th Anniversary Celebration, and the efforts of the hundreds of people who helped make this unique double anniversary year a once-in-a-lifetime experience.

In the following pages, we have tried to document what went into making the celebration happen—the people, resources, the sites, and the performances. Within these pages the anniversary year is visually captured in photographic essays of the major events. They provide the context, the sense of place, and the personality of our diverse programming schedule.

As the Anniversary Committee conducted its work, it became apparent that this yearlong effort was not just about the Borough having reached these benchmark anniversaries. To a greater extent, it was about Emmaus' people and the link between today's residents and those who had come before. In the process, there took place a remarkable bonding among members of the Anniversary Committee and the various task forces that were charged with planning the many activities.

The happy circumstance of the Borough receiving a second accolade from *Money* magazine as one of the Top 100 Small Towns in America only served to reinforce among the people of Emmaus a sense of special meaning and purpose. So, too, the wonderful 50th anniversary edition of the East Penn Press highlighted the more recent history of our Borough.

All came to a head during that remarkable August weekend as we came together in an outburst of happiness and pride, honoring our past, while celebrating who we are today. This could be seen in the faces of the many and diverse long-time Emmaus families who saw the significance of the celebration by coming out or returning from afar to revisit their past. This pride in being part of Emmaus's history clearly demonstrates the strength of this community, which is apparent as you peruse this book.

Many people have contributed to this publication. Without those who provided photographs and the histories of their organizations, this effort would have been a most difficult task. My colleagues on the Anniversary Book publication committee, Teri Sorg-McManamon, C. Richard Chartrand, and Corrine Durdock, provided vital assistance, whether researching, writing, and/or editing the text or in providing photographs of the various events. Designer Susan Eugster compiled sheets full of words and groups of photos and made them come alive on these pages. We owe a great debt of gratitude to Johanna Green, Marge Heatley, and Rodale, Inc. for staff assistance, and to TN Printing for the production of the book.

It has been a fantastic year in which we were allowed to look back and forward at the same time. Many good ideas were generated that our town fathers will take into account as we plan for our next 150 years. And, in so doing, they will build upon the labors of those who preceded them. It is to all those good people of Emmaus who stepped forward and helped lead the way that this book is dedicated.

Roger Whitcomb

{ **3**

STEERING COMMITTEE

Front row: Dr. Roger Whitcomb, Dave Faust, Craig Neely, Gene Clock, Atty. Audrey Racines, Marge Heatly, Johanna Green
Back row: Sam Landis, Jr., C. Richard Chartrand, Dr. John Kirschman, Dr. MIke Waddell, George Boyer, Lee Ann Gilbert, Martha Vines, Kathy Mintzer, Teri Sorg-McManamon, Teri Madison, Corrine Durdock
Missing: Steve Gould, Rev. Diane Joseph, Karen Servacek, Alison Hudak, Rev. Diane Joseph, Ruth Grohol

A Message from the Anniversary Committee

THE TOWN OF EMMAUS, founded by the Moravians, has been a very special place for many people over the past 250 years and, therefore, deserved a special celebration to commemorate 250 years as a community and 150 years as an incorporated borough. Plans for a celebration officially started on August 2, 2005, with Dr. John Kirschman at the helm to lay the groundwork. I assumed the reins from John on September 12, 2007, and continued the work of creating a yearlong celebration dedicated to having fun and making memories. There is much wonderful history about Emmaus and it will be said in the future that history was made in 2009.

The Emmaus 2009 Anniversary Committee was officially recognized as an all-volunteer sub-committee of the Emmaus Borough Council in 2008. It consisted of a Steering Committee that met regularly for more than two years and numerous Project Teams that had their own memberships dedicated to specific events. The names of these dedicated residents are listed later in this book. It's also important to note that this celebration would have been difficult if not impossible to facilitate without the consistent assistance that we received from local businesses, churches, school district, and the public works, police, fire, and ambulance departments of the Borough of Emmaus.

It has been my privilege and honor to chair the Anniversary Committee. Early in our planning we decided to make it a yearlong event, which is certainly what you would expect from persons residing, working, and volunteering in one of the Top 100 Places to Live in the United States! We had more than fifty different activities/events to join in throughout the year. Each and every activity/event was well planned and facilitated by the responsible Project Team, to the great enjoyment of all of us. No community could have done more than was done in Emmaus in 2009 to celebrate its historic roots, as well as move us boldly into the future. It truly was a privilege to witness the community coming together to make this celebration such a huge success.

On a personal note, it was one of the greatest experiences of my life because of the many wonderful people I met and had the pleasure of working with for several years. However, my experience was not unique. The common thread of numerous discussions among the many volunteers was how many new friends were made in the creation of this celebration.

My heartfelt thanks to everyone who participated in the many facets of this memorable year. This was a true team effort with everyone doing their best to make something special happen in the community that we all love. I truly hope that those who follow us in the future have as much fun and make as many memories as we did.

Dr. Mike Waddell,
CHAIRPERSON,
EMMAUS 2009 ANNIVERSARY CELEBRATION

{ 5

Anniversary Committee and Project Team Leaders

STEERING COMMITTEE

Mike Waddell, Chair

Teri Madison, 2nd Chair, Souvenirs, Web site

Roger Whitcomb, Treasurer, Budget & Finance, Government Relations, Fund-Raising, Publications

Nate Brown, Celebration Weekend

C. Richard Chartrand, Photo History & Documentation

Gene Clock, Celebration Weekend

Corrine Durdock, Press Relations, Publications

Dave Faust, Public Safety

Lee Ann Gilbert, Public Safety

Steve Gould, Brothers of the Brush

Johanna Green, Office Staff

Ruth Grohol, Centennial Belles

Marge Heatley, Office Staff

Rev. Diane Joseph, Moravian Church Love Feast

John Kirschman, Historian

Sam Landis, Facilities, Fireworks

Kathy Mintzer, Parade

Craig Neely, Time Capsules (1959 and 2009)

Audrey Racines, Legal

Karen Servacek, Office Staff

Teri Sorg-McManamon, Promotions & Marketing, Publications

Martha Vines, Volunteers

PROJECT TEAMS

6

Carl Arner, PA Dutch Play

Sandra Bachman, Emmaus Garden Club

Wes Barrett, Sound & Lighting

Bob Boehmer, Visual & Performing Arts

George Boyer, Musical Events

Janice Chartrand, Videography

Kathy Delhagen, Community Quilt Project

Tracy Dell, Emmaus Sentinels Drum & Bugle Corps

Bruce Denmead, Emmaus HS Band and Jazz Band

Brad Fogel, Emmaus Sentinels Drum & Bugle Corps

Eileen Frick, Emmaus Lioness Club

Tom Gettings, Wildlands Conservancy

Steve Gould, Brothers of the Brush

Ruth Grohol, Centennial Belles

Francis and Betty Lou Hartman, Emmaus Historical Society

Alan Hawman, Emmaus Heritage Alliance

Leslie Heffron, Visual & Performing Arts

Rev. Kevin Henning, Emmaus Moravian Church

Alison Hudak, Train Excursion Weekend

Rev. Diane Joseph, Moravian Church Love Feast

Jim Keller, Emmaus Lions Club

Ruth Kemmerer, Centennial Belles

Jeannette Lehman, Women's Club of Emmaus

Eric Loch, Train Excursion Weekend

Hagar Malone, Girl Scouts

Sandi Miklos, Emmaus Garden Club

Kathy Mintzer, Parade

Rich Musselman, PA Dutch Lessons

Rose Parry, Emmaus Garden Club

Rep. Doug Reichley, Legislature Liaison

Jo Sadrovitz, Concerts

John Schmoyer, Knauss Family Reunion

Bob Servacek, Special Displays

Rev. Canon Lexa Shallcross, Religious Services

Jeff Shubzda, Graphics

Denise Tempest, Educational Outreach

Carole Ann Trout, Emmaus Chorale

Judy Yanega, Emmaus Rotary Club

Snapshots

Special Treasures: 2009 Emmaus Anniversary Souvenirs

Very early in the celebration planning process, the Steering Committee recognized that the selection, collection, and sale of souvenirs would be a most welcome aspect of the anniversary memories. Souvenirs were purchased for sale throughout the year.

Commemorative Poster

In honor of Emmaus' unique milestones in 2009, the Emmaus Arts Commission created an official limited-edition commemorative poster. The poster is titled "Unforgettable Emmaus" and focuses on iconic symbols of Emmaus' history and the anniversary year. Proceeds from poster sales were earmarked to benefit the commission's programs.

Anniversary Celebration Parade

The August 15 anniversary parade featured several outstanding entries, including the Woodland String Band; the space shuttle replica, Blake, which carried the unearthed 1959 Time Capsule; a replica of a steam locomotive; a 1955 Woodson Dairy milk delivery truck; Forks of the Delaware Tin Lizzies antique cars; the reorganized Sentinels Alumni Drum and Bugle Corps; the Victorian Highwheelers; John Deere tractors from the East Central Pennsylvania Two-Cylinder Club; and numerous local bands and citizen marching units.

Space Shuttle "Blake"

The space shuttle "Blake," a unique mobile educational laboratory equipped with a microcomputer-networked learning environment equipped in a scrapped Marine Corps bus transformed into a state-of-the-art space classroom on wheels, appeared in the parade and was open for tours at the Saturday, August 15 Community Park activities. "Blake" is the brainchild of Emmaus Arts Commission President Robert Boehmer, an arts and science educator in the Parkland School District.

Arts Commission members wore special mission patch T-shirts and provided hands-on, out-of-this-world space art-related activities.

Train Excursion

As part of the yearlong celebration of the 250th Anniversary of Emmaus and sponsored by St. Luke's Hospital Network, the Emmaus 2009 Trains Committee hosted three days of passenger train excursions the weekend of October 3 to 5.

The trains departed from Kline's Lane off Main Street (near the Borough of Emmaus compost site) and continued southbound along the old Perkiomen Railroad line.

All trips traveled through the 1,798-foot Dillinger tunnel, constructed in 1875. The train was headed by two Reading FP7 passenger locomotives, built in 1950, restored and currently owned by the Reading Company Technical & Historical Society. The passenger coaches were on loan from the Morristown & Erie Railway in New Jersey.

Many exhibits were featured under the big white tent erected on the site.

Friday night featured a dinner and program following the train excursion.

The Train Committee offered the Emmaus 250th Year Anniversary HO gauge collectible train car, a replica of a Pennsylvania RR 1860 coach, for sale.

Anniversary Year in Review

THE PLANS FOR EMMAUS'S ANNIVERSARY CELEBRATION were four years in the making. The 2009 Anniversary Celebration's Steering Committee designed a logo with a train motif in keeping with the important role that railroads played and continue to play in the growth of the Borough.

The former police department headquarters in the lower level of Town Hall became the home of the 2009 Anniversary Celebration office. It was staffed by two dedicated volunteers, Marge Heatley and Johanna Green, who opened it on Wednesdays from 10 a.m. to 2 p.m. or by appointment.

Several projects using the anniversary logo were seen throughout town—stencils of the logo were drawn on the sidewalks, banners (purchased by individuals, businesses, and organizations) affixed to poles adorned the main streets, the Emmaus Flower Garden planted a landscape design near Weis Markets, the Emmaus Public Works staff created a design at the welcome sign near the library, and patriotic bows donated by Jackie Owens were hung throughout the downtown.

Several activites were ongoing throughout 2009:

- Photographer Rich Chartrand prepared a changing monthly slide show at the Emmaus Public Library. Photos were courtesy of Mr. Chartrand's and the Emmaus Historical Society collections. Presentations included past celebrations, the Triangle, borough government, churches, police department, businesses, industry, schools, fire department, veterans, and the Time Capsule.

- The East Penn Press published a weekly Trivia Item that was gleaned from the 50 years of the paper's publications.

- Work on a 250th Anniversary Commemorative Quilt began in May and was unveiled in September during Heritage Days. The quilt, conceived and coordinated by Kathy Delhagen, a well-known local quilting artist, included donated items stitched together in a "crazy quilt" fashion—a style very popular in the late 1800s. More than 150 sentimental contributions from individuals and groups are part of the finished quilt, which was loaned to the Emmaus Public Library. Plans are for it to be displayed at the Emmaus Historical Society. A booklet containing photos of the finished blocks and descriptions of the donated items is available at the library and historical society.

- To announce the news of the Anniversary Celebration, two designated town criers, C. Richard Chartrand and Steve Gould, dressed in Moravian garb and rang the traditional bell proclaiming "important news" at several churches in December 2008. Throughout the 2009 anniversary year itself, Chartrand took on the role of official town crier, appearing at many of the activites.

Corrine Durdock

9

Timeline

JANUARY

January 3: The Kick-Off Celebration, "Party Like It's 1959," took place at 8 p.m. at the VFW, 316 Main Street.

January 21: Local architect Alan Hawman presented a lecture, "A Walking Tour of Emmaus", at the Emmaus Public Library, 11 E. Main Street.

FEBRUARY

February: Richard Musselman organized Pennsylvania Dutch classes through the East Penn School District.

February 7 and 8: The Emmaus Arts Commission coordinated the Snowblast Winter Festival held at various venues throughout the Borough. An ice sculpture featured the 2009 Emmaus Anniversary logo.

February 7: The first of several South Mountain hikes held throughout the year were organized by the Wildlands Conservancy. Hikes formed at the Alpine Street entrance.

February 18: The Emmaus Historical Society presented a slide show featuring photos of the 1959 and 1984 Emmaus anniversary parades. Pat Zentner, granddaughter of the owners of the Broad Street Hotel and Opera House, was a presenter.

February 19: Dr. John Kirschman presented a lecture on "The 250 Year History of Emmaus" at the Emmaus Public Library.

February 24: The Emmaus Main Street Program held its Faschnacht & Forsythia Festival at St. John's United Church of Christ, 139 N. Fourth Street.

Timeline

MARCH

March 18: Dr. Bruce Rowell presented a lecture, "The Geological History of Emmaus," at the Emmaus Public Library.

March 26: Wendy S. Weida presented a lecture, "The Early History of Emmaus," at the Emmaus Historical Society meeting, St. John's Lutheran Church, Fifth and Chestnut Streets.

APRIL

April 15: Martha Capwell Fox presented a lecture, "Early Silk Mills of Emmaus and the Lehigh Valley," at the Emmaus Historical Society meeting.

April 18: The Shelter House Society held its annual Patriots' Day Dinner honoring early Emmaus history at the Emmaus Moravian Church Fellowship Hall.

April 25: The Wildlands Conservancy held its second in a series of South Mountain hikes.

MAY

May 7: The Kiwanis Club held its 36th annual pancake breakfast at Fire Company #1. This year's fundraiser was dedicated to celebrating "Unforgettable Emmaus."

Sundays: The Emmaus Farmers' Market opened at the KNBT parking lot, Main Street. Anniversary groups, Brothers of the Brush and Centennial Belles, held registrations for the beard-growing and costume contests to be judged during the Grand Celebration weekend.

May 20: Douglas Peters presented a program, "Transportation in Emmaus," which was organized by the Emmaus Historical Society.

Faschnacht
Forsythia Festival

Timeline

MAY—*continued*

May 24: The Emmaus Commemorative Gardens Foundation organized a Veterans Commemorative Brick Installation. The foundation installed a special brick to commemorate the service of all veterans from the Emmaus community.

JUNE

June 14: The Emmaus Flag Day Association (EFDA) held its Flag Day program in Emmaus Community Park. Featured were a performance by the Emmaus Chorale, a Flag Day proclamation by Emmaus Mayor Winfield Iobst, and the winners of the student Poetry and Essay contests. The EFDA held its annual banquet meeting earlier in June.

June 20: The Emmaus Garden Club held its semi-annual flower show at St. John's Lutheran Church, titled "Our Rich Heritage."

June 20: The Arts Commission organized its annual Art in the Garden, "Our Rich Heritage." The event was held at various gardens in Emmaus.

June 20: Emmaus Moravian Church held a Lovefeast, in celebration of people uniting together in compassion.

June 21: The Emmaus Chorale's rescheduled concert, "Music Is Always There," was held at the Lutheran Church of the Holy Spirit, 3461 S. Cedar Crest Blvd. The concert featured Moravian music and tunes from "Showboat."

14

Timeline

JULY

July 17 and 18: Knauss family descendents convened in Emmaus for the Knauss family's first reunion since the 1920s. The 2009 reunion was planned to coincide with Emmaus' 2009 yearlong anniversary celebrations. Visitors came from Washington, Arizona, Wisconsin, California, Maine, Massachusetts, Indiana, and Michigan.

Late July: The Borough published a special Newsletter that listed all the events for the Grand Celebration weekend.

AUGUST

August 14, 15, and 16: Emmaus 250th Anniversary Weekend Celebration. The three-day celebration included opening ceremonies under a tent near the Triangle, dedication of the newly reconstructed Triangle, and an anniversary parade, which included the debut of the Emmaus Sentinels Alumni Drum and Bugle Corps. The Corps, which had disbanded in the 1970s, was reorganized as part of the Anniversary Celebration. The post office offered an anniversary postmark made available at a kiosk near the Triangle. Family and class reunions were held at Emmaus Community Park, along with various other activities. The 1959 Time Capsule was opened. The traditional Trombone Choir church service was held at God's Acre Cemetery, and an ecumenical church service was held at St. Ann's Catholic Church. Closing ceremonies were held at Emmaus High School's football field, followed by a memorable fireworks display.

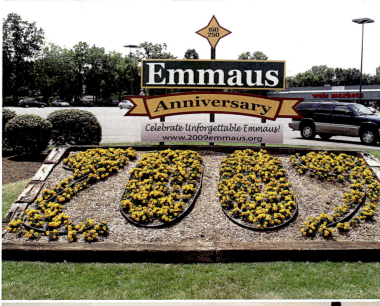

Timeline

SEPTEMBER

September 11: The Emmaus Public Library held its annual Heroes Night to honor the men and women who keep our community safe.

September 11 and 12: Emmaus Heritage Days Celebration, organized by the Main Street Program, was held at various venues throughout the Borough. The 1803 House held a "Restoration Reunion," honoring former contributors to the restoration of the historic property. The Shelter House debuted its new children's book, *Discovering the Shelter House—Toby's Tale*, written by Corrine Durdock, to commemorate the Borough's 150th and 250th anniversaries. A new event, Emmaus 2009 Wildlife Art Festival, a collaboration of the Wildlands Conservancy, and the Emmaus Arts Commission, was held on September 11, showcasing the Lehigh Valley's award-winning nature and wildlife artists, environmental groups, and animal preservation officers.

September 19: The Shops of Emmaus kicked off its annual scarecrow contest. Some of the scarecrows were dressed in period costume in keeping with the Borough's Anniversary Celebration.

September 19: Huffs Union Church players presented a Pennsylvania Dutch play, "Shtimerei" (Election), a Carl Arner original three-act comedy in the Pennsylvania Dutch dialect, at St. John's Lutheran Church.

September 30: The Emmaus Heritage Alliance held a workshop, "Your Old House Workshop," to help participants identify the age and architectural style of their homes.

EMMAUS
COMMUNITY
PARK

Timeline

OCTOBER

October 2, 3, and 4: The 2009 Train Committee organized train excursions. The ride on a '50s-era diesel train took participants through the Dillinger Tunnel. Friday night attendees enjoyed a train ride and a catered dinner under a tent next to the railroad tracks.

October 18: The Emmaus Arts Commission held its 5th annual Student Horror Film Festival. Students were given ninety-six hours to create, shoot and edit a six-minute film for cash and prizes. The event featured a connection to the 250th Anniversary Celebration. Winners were announced at Eyer Middle School.

October 31: The Emmaus Police Department hosted an Open House to commemorate its 100th anniversary.

NOVEMBER

November 13: As part of the December 3–5 Emmaus Old-Fashioned Christmas celebration, the Main Street Program held a storefront-decorating contest. The theme was "Anniversary Holiday in Emmaus." The participants were encouraged to incorporate the official Emmaus Anniversary Logo in their design.

DECEMBER

December 3, 4, and 5: Emmaus celebrated its annual Old-Fashioned Christmas. Organized by the Emmaus Main Street Program, it was held at various venues throughout the community. Among the events was a concert, "Emmaus 2009 Anniversary Finale," at Bethel Bible Fellowship Church, featuring the Emmaus Chorale and performers from the Seven Generations Charter School. The lighting of the borough's Christmas tree was held on the newly renovated Triangle. The Shops of Emmaus held its "Toast the Holidays" with activities. On December 5, the Time Capsule to be opened in 2059 was buried at 10 a.m. on the Emmaus Library grounds.

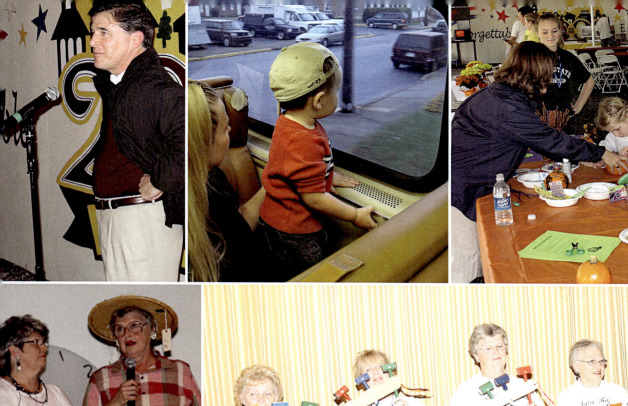

The Celebration Weekend

AS THE 2009 CELEBRATION PROGRESSED, the town eagerly anticipated the Grand Celebration weekend, August 14th to 16th, when the years of planning would culminate in three days of events and activites. The Party on the Triangle on Friday night attracted thousands to the downtown, while Saturday began with the Anniversary Parade through town and continued with Community Park hosting picnics, class reunions, food vendors, opening and display of the 1959 Time Capsule, Brothers of the Brush shave-off, presentation of the Centennial Belles, and an exhibit featuring a half-size replica of the Space Shuttle. The weekend ended with an aptly spectacular fireworks display, the likes of which were never seen before. The Grand Celebration weekend proved to be the gem of 2009, with residents, visitors, families, and friends feeling the pride in community that makes Emmaus a town of distinction.

{ 23

The Time Capsule

I AM PREPARING TO SEAL THE TIME CAPSULE. It is with the deepest of emotions that I am writing to you. As you will learn, a time capsule is a journey of introspection. I volunteered to chair the 2009 Time Capsule Committee because I thought that it would be fun. It was, but it was much more than that.

I stood at the Emmaus Triangle as we dug to find it, and when the backhoe bucket hit something solid I could feel the tingling all the way down my spine. We pulled back the top of the concrete vault and I almost cried when I caught just a glimpse of the 1959 Time Capsule. Suddenly, its importance became magnified. The moment was not just a moment, it transcended fifty years. I could almost feel the past as we strapped the Capsule and lifted it out of its tomb.

When we opened the Capsule in the privacy of the Emmaus Town Hall garage in May, the Time Capsule Committee anticipated nothing more than a mundane cursory inventory of the items to ascertain their integrity, as we had no clue about whether the items would be intact. When we opened the Capsule and began perusing its contents, something magical happened. We were transported to another era. The immaculately preserved photos painted a beautiful picture of Emmaus in 1959, so much so that we could feel the spirit of the 1959 Anniversary Celebration.

Having Mayor Iobst there made the experience even more special. When he looked at his father's picture and commented how his father was the mayor in 1959, it was almost surreal. There could have been no closer connection to the past—which defines the purpose of a time capsule. Hollywood could not have scripted anything more appropriate. The experience was almost numbing, causing deep introspection by the Committee, thinking about themselves, the community, and the comparisons of the past and the present.

We were excited on August 15 and 16 when we opened the Time Capsule for the public and displayed all of its contents at Community Park. We estimated that at least 1,500 people passed through the display, at which every item was made available to, and could be touched by, the public.

The Time Capsule Committee believed that history needs to be felt to be most appreciated. Kids touched mementos from the 1959 Celebration, while adults read newspapers from 1959. We handed out 1959 commemorative stamps that were in the Time Capsule so that they could become cherished family heirlooms. We distributed the crumbled packing newspapers to the public attending the opening ceremony so that they could return home with a piece of history.

Today we are burying the 2009 Time Capsule. We are confident that the 2059 Time Capsule Committee will experience a journey similar to ours. We want to thank the entire Emmaus community for making 2009 a very special year when we all learned just how close a community we have.

Craig Neely
EMMAUS BOROUGH MANAGER

Business and Community Histories

IN 2008, CALL WENT OUT to Borough businesses and civic organizations to submit histories of their groups for publication in a future commemorative book. Not all those contacted did so, despite repeated announcements. Nevertheless, we are pleased to offer the following business and community organizations.

Acupuncture & Oriental Medicine

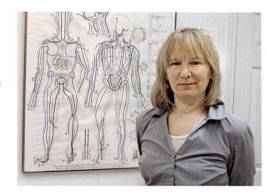

Lisa Baas's complementary health care practice has its early roots in Emmaus. After being a tour guide at the Rodale Farm on Cedar Crest Boulevard and working at Food Naturally on 3rd and Main Streets as a macrobiotic chef, Lisa began her healing practice as a shiatsu massage therapist, dietary counselor, and mind-body medicine practitioner.

Her practice in Emmaus includes Acupuncture & Oriental Medicine. Lisa is a licensed acupuncturist and herbalist, offering acupuncture, acupressure massage therapy, dietary counseling, lifestyle coaching, meditation, rehabilitation exercises, herbal and homeopathic medicines, and more.

Alternative Healthcare

Dr. Merlin Haas is the owner of Alternative Healthcare at 860 Broad Street in Emmaus. Dr. Haas has been in practice for thirty years since his graduation from Palmer Chiropractic School in 1979; he settled at the Broad Street office with his wife Donna, in 2006.

In 1994, he added the degree of naturopathic practitioner to his resume. Dr. Haas has a strong passion and belief that herbs and vitamins can heal a body. Dr. Haas also has unique ability to work with energy testing called Contact Reflex Analysis, a form of kinesiology. Using an old-fashioned hands-on approach combining both chiropractic and Contact Reflex Analysis, his practice has grown quickly, with many of his patients have become good friends, like an extended family.

Air Products

Air Products was founded by the late Leonard P. Pool in 1940. From its beginnings in Detroit, Michigan, the company moved to Chattanooga, Tennessee, and in 1946 set up operations at the former Donaldson Iron Works in Emmaus. Today its corporate headquarters is located on a 600-acre campus in Trexlertown.

Air Products serves customers in industrial, energy, technology, and healthcare markets around the world, marketing atmospheric gases, making semiconductors faster and displays brighter with its electronic chemicals, and manufacturing coatings and adhesives in a more environmentally friendly manner with its performance materials. Recognized for its innovative culture, operational excellence, and commitment to safety and the environment, Air Products has operations in more than forty countries and employs 22,000 employees around the globe.

American Millwork and Cabinetry

American Millwork and Cabinetry was initially conceived in Quakertown, though in 2006, it had the misfortune of experiencing a devastating fire that totally destroyed the shop. The company was able to relocate to its current Broad Street location.

Thankfully, area business owners, political figures, and Emmaus Borough have been extremely helpful in assisting with their transition into the community. Lehigh Valley Economic Development Corporation (LVEDC) enabled this company to grow and employ more people from the community than ever before.

Being a merit company and an active member of Associated Builders and Contractors of America (ABC) has allowed us to continue on a path toward greater employment for Emmaus and the Lehigh Valley. The work ethic in the Emmaus community is old world, as is the type of architectural millwork and cabinetry American Millwork and Cabinetry produces every day.

Audrey Gardner Racines, Attorney-at-Law

Audrey Gardner Racines began practicing law forty years ago with her father, Theodore R. Gardner, and her brother, James Knoll Gardner. After her brother, who is now a federal judge, became a Common Pleas Judge in 1981, the firm became Gardner, Racines, and Sheetz and has continued to engage in the general practice of law.

Mrs. Racines restricts her practice to wills and estates, and in 2007 she was joined in her practice by her daughter Amanda Racines Lovett.

Emmaus Mercantile Club

The original charter of the Emmaus Mercantile Club was granted in March 1908 to fifty-five residents, twenty-seven nonresidents, and two honorary members, beginning operations on May 4, 1908, in the old Hanna Cigar Factory at 425-429 Railroad Street. The club was established as a private members-only club and was restricted to Emmaus merchants, businessmen, and other professionals.

Membership has evolved from the strictly enforced mix mentioned above to the current day friends and associates of the Lehigh Valley. "The Merc" is still the place to come for gatherings and relaxation, in addition to great meals and good entertainment.

In the last fifteen years numerous improvements were completed: a new and larger bar area, new kitchen cooking equipment, new parking lot, and various building improvements to the original building.

On Saturday May 7, 2008, "The Merc" celebrated its 100th year with a New Year's Eve type gala. A calendar of events and pictures of the building and patrons were distributed to all 3,500+ members.

John M. Ashcraft III, Attorney-at-Law

{ 33

John M. Ashcraft III graduated from Emmaus High School in 1968. He left the area to complete his undergraduate and juris doctor degrees, returning in 1975. Since then he has practiced civil law in Lehigh County, serving clients primarily in the areas of wills, estates, business law, real estate, zoning, personal injury, and domestic relations.

He moved his office to 20 North 5th Street in the Borough in April 2009. His office operates with two part-time assistants to help provide a human voice response to inquiring callers. Attorney Ashcraft aims to explain not just what law applies to client situations, but also how laws operate and the policies behind them—in plain English.

Discovery Preschool

Discovery Preschool began its Early Childhood Education facility in Emmaus in October 1984. Wanting to be a resource for working parents with small children, the old Art Schneck Optical one-story building on North Street was purchased and was then converted to a nursery school for ages three to six years.

The preschool grew and a second floor was added. Additional educational services were added, including state-certified full-day Kindergarten and preschool programs. Responding to requests for before- and after-school care for school-age children that attend Lincoln and Jefferson Elementary Schools and for infant care from parents who had other children in our preschool classes, the infant room was opened in 1990 and an after-school program began.

Dries and Reichard, Inc.

Dries and Reichard, Inc. was founded in 1935 as a coal company by David S. and Irwin C. Dries. In 1955, they began to deliver fuel oil. By 1970, William Reichard had become a partner. In 1973 the company began offering oil.

The company has always been a family-run business, with William Reichard as head of the company, wife, Eleanor, running the office, and son Scott in charge of oil deliveries.

The Reichards have retired from active participation but have left the management in the capable hands of Debbie and Steve Frey. Dries and Reichard is always expanding, delivering all of the services that the big city companies offer, yet keeping the small town personal service that so many in the Emmaus area expect.

East Penn Bank

East Penn Bank received its charter on November 6, 1990, and opened its doors in early 1991 at 731 Chestnut Street. Brent L. Peters, president and CEO of East Penn Bank, and the founding board of directors sensed the need for a community-focused, locally owned bank in the Emmaus area. In 2004, 2005, and 2007, it was ranked by *US Banker* magazine, as one of the country's Top 200 Community Banks. When East Penn Bank merged with Harleysville National Bank in November 2007, it had nine branches and more than one hundred forty employees. As 2009 came to a close, the bank served the region with nineteen locations in Lehigh, Northampton, Berks, Carbon, and Monroe counties, with assets in excess of $900 million. In late 2009, the Harleysville Group was acquired by Niagara Bank of New York.

Eisenhard's Decorating Center

Eisenhard's Decorating Center has been committed to quality products and service throughout the Lehigh Valley since 1952. Founded by Al and Jake Eisenhard, it was one of the first businesses to occupy the southeast end of Emmaus. Although they installed many flooring surfaces, Eisenhards became known as a top-quality store for vinyl floor-covering installation. In 1977, current owner Joseph Kunkler purchased the business and opted to keep its original name due to its esteemed reputation. Eisenhard's expanded to become a full-fledged decorating center, offering decorating solutions for floors, windows, and walls. Its building underwent dramatic changes including extending the showroom to include a lower-level showroom and also equipping Eisenhard's with more office space and a larger warehouse.

Emmaus Village

In 1908 a home was built at 659 Broad Street in Emmaus. Since the beginning, it has been a loving home for older adults in town. Some remember it as Manco Manor. In 2003, Northampton Village Inc. turned this community into Emmaus Village. Its mission is to help their residents maximize their independence in a safe and caring homelike environment. The staff is dedicated to providing loving, respectful care to each resident. The goal is to meet the physical, social, and spiritual needs of those individuals who have chosen to make their home with us. In December 2006, they added "Inspirations," a secured memory-impaired unit. It is a special care unit named for the inspiration that this tradition has given its staff. The goal is to inspire a lifestyle where independence with assistance can be maintained regardless of the residents' cognitive abilities.

East Penn Press

The *East Penn Press* began in Emmaus through the efforts of Gladys Dreisbach, owner of the Emmaus Jewel Shop, who started her business in Emmaus in 1946. With the borough's Centennial celebration planned for 1959, Dreisbach was joined in her efforts by Bill Stoler, who owned a photography shop on the triangle, to start an Emmaus newspaper.

Charles Meredith III, owner and publisher of *The Free Press* in Quakertown, agreed to publish an Emmaus weekly newspaper and on April 9, 1959, the first issue of the *Emmaus Free Press* hit the streets at 10 cents a copy.

The newspaper occupied several offices in Emmaus until 1987. In October 1987, shortly after Pencor Services, which published the *Times-News* in Lehighton, purchased the paper from the Merediths, the office moved to 10 S. 4th Street, Emmaus. On July 8, 1992, the office relocated to its current address, 1633 N. 26th Street, South Whitehall Township, which it shares with its sister publications: the *Parkland Press*, the *Northwestern Press*, the *Whitehall-Coplay Press*, the *Northampton Press*, the *Salisbury Press,* and the *Catasauqua Press*. The *Bethlehem Press'* editorial offices are located in Bethlehem.

The East Penn Press celebrated its 50-year anniversary in April 2009. Through 50 years, the paper has continued to serve the community with local news. Its management has always recognized that the local support from advertisers and readers is its recipe for success.

Emmaus Bakery

Emmaus Bakery was conceived in 1934 by John Sadler, who operated it for nineteen years. In 1953, John and Mary Piszchek bought the business and ran it for ten years until they leased it to Jeanella "Jean" Zayaitz. During Jean's tenure, she had her son Richard Sr. work closely by her side, teaching him the baking business. By 1968, Mr. Piszchek and Jean Zayaitz stepped aside, selling the business to Richard Sr, who, with his wife Marjorie, continued the family baking traditions handed down from his mother. As Richard Sr.'s mother did, he passed the trade along to his son, also named Richard, who purchased the business from his father in 1984.

Richard, known as "Rick", continues to use his grandmother Nanna's recipes. From the smell of cookies and bear claws, to the breads and doughnuts or a cake for any occasion, you can be sure that the quality and consistency come from homemade ingredients.

Fretz Realty, Inc.

Fretz Realty Inc. was established by J. Erwin Fretz in 1949. He worked from the living room of his home on Fourth Street in Emmaus before building at the present location at 188 Jefferson Street. In 1953, Erwin formed a partnership with his brother, Harvey D. Fretz. In subsequent years Erwin's two sons, Glenn and David, joined the business, followed by Harvey's son, John.

The Fretz family has always taken its commitment to outstanding and professional service very seriously. Fretz Realty has served as a friendly neighbor to Emmaus residents, occupying the same location for fifty years, and is known to have a welcoming open-door policy where you very likely will be greeted by one of the Fretz's.

George's Greenhouse

George's Greenhouse was founded in 1921 by Lee George's great grandfather and is currently owned and operated by Lee as a fourth-generation florist. They have been at 183 Ridge Street in Emmaus, since 1977. The shop is on the 1st floor of a two-story building in a residential neighborhood one block from the main shopping area. George's Greenhouse is a full-service florist for all floral occasions, serving Emmaus, Macungie, Allentown, Zionsville, Trexlertown, Alburtis, Wescosville, and Vera Cruz. They also offer wire service and international orders.

Granny Schmidt's Custom Cake Shop

Granny Schmidt's bakery opened in September 2006 to bring best-in-class bakery products to customers who enjoy the marriage of high style and century-old goodness. They make every cake from scratch, often one at a time, using nothing you wouldn't have found at the corner grocery a hundred years ago.

Recipes are designed for flavor and texture, not for ease of handling, structural strength, or shelf life.

Granny Schmidt's is owned by Art Schmidt, Jr. and Michelle Quier. Pastry Chef Samantha Kish earned her degree from Johnson & Wales University.

Harned-Durham Energy

In 1954, Harned-Durham Oil Company, Inc., under the guidance of Fred S. Durham and William B. Harned, began as a Sinclair distributor in nearby Macungie. In 1973, Ralf V. Harned constructed a new building and half-million gallon fuel tank on Buckeye Road near Emmaus and soon added garages to house delivery and service trucks.

In the early 1980s, Ralf's son, Michael Harned, formed Oil Discounters, a company designed to offer fuel at a discounted price to customers who did not desire full service. In the 2000s, Michael added onto the existing office bulding, renovated the interior, and renamed the company Harned-Durham Energy. Harned-Durham serves all of the Emmaus and surrounding areas.

37

Iobst Travel Service/American Express

The year was 1979; the place Emmaus, Pennsylvania; the location, the center of town at "the Triangle," and Maryellen Iobst had a plan to open a travel agency in Emmaus. A local airline representative asked, "Why a travel agency in Emmaus, Pennsylvania?" Maryellen's response, "With a name like Iobst, where else would I open a travel agency?"

Iobst Travel opened on the Triangle in Emmaus on September 4, 1979, with Maryellen and one employee. Iobst Travel became an American Express Representative in 2004 and developed a wide variety of products to serve its clientele. By 2009, Iobst Travel employed several individuals and twenty independent contractors. The agency offers foreign currency exchanges as well as card benefits for its clients and is a strong supplier base for cruise lines.

Jacqueline Owens Beauty Boutique

In 1988, Jacqueline Owens opened a salon at 31 N. Third Street. Jacqueline Owens Beauty Boutique is a complete salon, offering cuts, perms, colors, foils, painting, and so on. It's a lively environment where clients are treated like family. They welcome customers of every age. The stylists are friendly, caring, and happy to help you look your best. JoLinda Buss has worked there for twenty-three years. Debra Helfrich joined in 1998. To keep up with current trends, Jacqueline takes continuing education classes in New York City and belongs to the International Hairdressers and the local Hairdressers Associations.

JoAnne's Styling Salon

After more than forty-two years in the business and at the age of sixty-two, JoAnne Amig achieved one of her goals in life—to own a hair salon. In January 2004, she opened JoAnne's Styling Salon at 1245 Chestnut Street in Emmaus to cheering loyal customers. Her clients range in age from nine months to ninety-two years old. JoAnne's philosophy is to work with her clients' natural beauty, listen to the customer, and advise them so they can achieve the style they desire.

She knew since high school that she wanted to be a hairdresser, and she graduated from beauty school in 1962. In addition to being sole proprietor of the salon, JoAnne also sits on the Cosmetology Occupational Advisory Council of the Lehigh Career & Technical Institute. She attends classes and trade shows, which allow her to increase her knowledge and keep up with the new trends.

KNBT Bank

KNBT was formed in 2003 when Keystone Savings Bank merged with Nazareth Bank. In January 2008, KNBT merged with National Penn Bancshares, Inc., and is the largest division of the organization with fifty-six offices throughout six counties.

An offering of a wide spectrum of high-quality financial products and services to its customers has helped KNBT rank as the number one bank in Northampton County and number two in Lehigh County in deposit market share. KNBT, named Best of the Valley© in *Lehigh Valley Magazine's* 13th annual readers' survey, also places a high priority on the economic growth and vitality of its market area by supporting local civic, charitable, and cultural organizations.

Kinder Castle Child Care

Kinder Castle Child Care was started in April 1993 by Charles and Joyce Nearhouse. They purchased two centers, one on State Avenue and one on Harrison Street and served infants through school-aged children. In 2004, they downsized by selling one center and concentrated on school-age children.

Charlie is a retired letter carrier and teaches the children to play chess. Joyce has spent years working with special needs children and teaches the children to sew. Their daughter, Angel Avery, has served as director since 1993.

Laudenslager Insurance Agency

Laudenslager Insurance Agency was started in Emmaus in 1932 by Norman and Minnie Laudenslager. This third-generation business has continued to provide service and a personal touch to its clients. Burton Laudenslager continued the business, providing property, casualty, and commercial insurance, tax preparation, bookkeeping, payroll and notary service until 1995. Now his daughter, Carol Laudenslager, continues the family tradition.

As Carol says, "we always go out of our way to provide the personal touch, so we stand out from most insurance agencies." It now offers life insurance, annuities, and long-term care insurance providing customers with a truly "one-stop" shopping experience.

{ 39

Once Is Not Enuff

Once Is Not Enuff was established by Sally McGovern in 1976 and moved to Emmaus in 1978. In 1989, Nancy Owen purchased it and operates at the same location, on the Triangle at 4th and Main Streets.

The shop features designer and quality clothing for women for a fraction of retail prices. Consignors sell their gently used items and receive 50 per cent of the selling price—a win for everyone and a natural way to recycle and help the environment.

Shoppers find everything from lovely gowns to everyday casual clothing and any accessory imaginable. The shop is open seven days a week for everyone's convenience.

Parkway Printing

Ron Billman opened Parkway Printing's doors in April 1993. Located in Allentown for fourteen years, it moved to Emmaus in July 2007. "It was a rather smooth transition for me," Ron says. "I have been a resident of Emmaus for thirty-four years and raised my family here. I knew it was the place to move my business." Tara (Prutsman) Mohr, the company's graphic designer and digital printing specialist, is a lifelong resident of Emmaus.

This full service commercial printer specializes in graphic design, business forms consulting, offset printing, and digital printing. Ron and Tara are thrilled to work with Emmaus businesses and individuals and look forward to many years serving the Emmaus community.

Penn Contractors

Intelligent, innovative design; elegant materials; and superior construction standards are the keystones of a successful building project. They are also the keystones around which Penn Contractors has built its reputation. Penn Contractors was founded in 1990 to meet a need for high-end, one-of-a-kind remodeling and renovation.

Its goal—to meet both aesthetic and budget expectations—is achieved through watchful, hands-on management at every stage. From architectural design through material selection and up to construction, customers enjoy working with a team of professionals who attend to every detail.

Prestige Marble & Granite

Ingenuity, common sense, and trendsetting describe Prestige Marble & Granite. Incorporated in October 2000 and officially open for business in Emmaus on February 17, 2001, Prestige began blazing the trail for a new way of presenting and fabricating stone, quartz, and solid surface countertops in the marketplace. A well-organized and well-stocked showroom staffed with specialized sales professionals and a nearby state-of-the-art fabrication shop has proven to be a winning combination for customers purchasing countertops and tile in a comfortable and user-friendly setting.

After several years, its shop expanded to a 45,000-square-foot facility one block from Chestnut Street. In September 2008, the showroom took over a newly designed 15,000-square-foot home at the end of the "Auto Mile," featuring a stone selection center with more than forty full countertop displays and approximately 300 on-site slabs.

Richards Jewelers

Richards Jewelers began in Hellertown, Pennsylvania, in 1971 and moved its office in 1976 to the old Merritt Lumber building on Chestnut Street in Emmaus. It has specialized in selling and repairing jewelry and watches. Richards Jewelers has enjoyed its Emmaus location because of the small town atmosphere, which has allowed the business to be a successful jewelry store.

Service Master Clean

ServiceMaster Clean is proud of having been part of the Emmaus community for thirty-three years. Scott and Freda Witmer moved their cleaning franchise to Emmaus in 1976. From its 933 Chestnut Street location, ServiceMaster crews are dispatched to help keep community homes and offices clean and healthy inside and outside.

The business was established in 1967 by Scott's father, Glenn. It was franchised that same year and transferred to Scott's ownership in 1975.

Specially trained and equipped technicians clean walls, floors, carpets, furniture, and drapery; wash siding, walks, windows; and clean/seal decks and fences. ServiceMaster crews provide mitigation services after casualty events. Additionally, its janitorial teams provide contract routine maintenance services in commercial buildings.

Law Offices of John O. Stover Jr.

In August 1985, after having practiced law in Allentown for seven years, John (Jack) Stover opened his solo general practice at 537 Chestnut Street, Emmaus. According to Jack, "I opened my practice because of my wish to relocate from Allentown to Emmaus, and to practice as a solo practitioner in my hometown. I thoroughly enjoy problem solving, which is the primary nature of my business, as well as working in the 'small town' atmosphere of Emmaus."

Jack's practice has evolved to include elder law, estate planning and administration, business law, zoning, and real estate. Preparing wills, trusts, powers of attorneys, and living wills have become an important part of his practice.

Sweet Memories

Take one historic property in beautiful Emmaus, add in one creative, hardworking family with big ideas, stir in great customers, wonderful food, lots of atmosphere, a charming gift shop, irresistible baked goods, and a lot of attention to detail, and you have the recipe for success at Sweet Memories.

In 1994, Mark and Jamie Smith opened a small family business that offered the best food and pastries in a restaurant with lots of charm. They later added a gift shop so it would be a special place to spend an afternoon.

There have been changes along the way. The restaurant has grown, the hours have expanded, and the gift shop is now a destination on its own. The food is still made fresh every day; the bakery still offers the homemade, old-fashioned desserts. Sunday Brunch is a favorite. Foremost, Mark and Jamie Smith are there every day ready to make you feel at home.

Thermoplastic Valves Inc

Incorporated in 1980, Thermoplastic Valves Inc. (TVI) is a master distributor of plastic valves. A move to 53 S. 7th Street in Emmaus took place in 1990. In 1996, it began occupying the former Homespun Weavers, for a total warehouse of 10,000 sq. ft. TVI has six regional sales engineers along with stocking distributors throughout the United States, parts of Canada, Mexico, the Caribbean, and South America.

TVI services industries that require complete resistance to corrosion and contamination in both metal and plastic piping systems, such as water filtration, water purification, wastewater filtration, de-ionized water, agriculture, including irrigation, fertilization and pesticide applications, aquaculture, mining, pharmaceuticals, chemical processing, swimming pools and spas, aquariums, the photographic industry, metal finishing, food processing, paper processing, petro-chemical, fluid circulation stems, and original equipment manufactured products.

East Penn Animal Hospital

Dr. Stewart Rockwell opened East Penn Animal Hospital in 1951 on State Avenue, treating large and small animals. In 1955, Dr. Rockwell moved his practice to its current location at 1020 Chestnut Street.

The practice grew with the addition of Drs. Wayne Hachten and Mohamed Eid. Gloria Hieter joined the practice in 1977 as a technician and has served in various roles. In 1978, Dr. Rockwell sold the practice to Dr. Eid and retired knowing that his practice would be in good hands. Dr. Eid ran the practice for twenty-two years before selling it to Healthy Pet in 2000. In 2001, Renae Tallman joined the practice and is currently the manager.

East Penn Animal Hospital continues to treat small and exotic animals.

Wesley Works Real Estate

The Wesley Works name has evolved many times since its founder, Wesley Barrett, initially used this name in 1987 when he started his first "business"—Wesley Works Snow Removal. Since then the name has been altered to fit an ever-growing collection of small businesses. After almost twenty years of growth and expansion, Wesley Works needed a new larger home for its business and officially moved into downtown Emmaus in July 2008. Today Wesley Works focuses on three main businesses: Real Estate, Wedding and Studio Photography, and DJ Entertainment. The 500 Chestnut Street office includes a photo studio, conference rooms, private and common offices and retains much of the historic charm its original owners intended.

{ 43

Rodale Inc.

Rodale an integral part in Emmaus' growth

THERE ARE MANY BUSINESSES AND PEOPLE who have a long history in Emmaus. Rodale Press or as it's known today, Rodale Inc., is one of them. With a multitude of properties in Emmaus and hundreds of employees working in the Borough, Rodale has had a huge economic impact on the area.

In this book celebrating Emmaus' 150 years of incorporation as a borough and 250 years as a community, it seems fitting to recognize the contributions of the family and business that has played an integral role in Emmaus' history.

It has been almost 80 years since the name Rodale first appeared in the Emmaus area. J. I. (Jerome Irving) Rodale and his brother, Joe, moved their electrical wiring manufacturing business to Emmaus in 1930. Its success enabled J. I. to go into the publishing business. By 1942, Rodale Press launched its first successful magazine, *Organic Farming and Gardening,* and in 1950, the first issue of *Prevention* was published.

J.I. believed that there was a direct relationship between the declining health of America's soil and the health of America's people. He put his theories into practice on a 60-acre farm near Emmaus, which is now the site of the Working Tree Center. J.I.'s ideas slowly took root and spread. Today, he is widely recognized as the father of the organic movement in America.

Following J.I.'s death in 1971, his son, Bob, who had been president since 1951, took over the leadership of the company. Rodale grew into the strong, positive force it is today, spreading the message "You can do it" across the pages of numerous books and magazines, reflecting the philosophy that people really can take charge of their own lives and their health.

Bob expanded farm and health research with the purchase of a 333-acre farm near Kutztown, establishing what is now the Rodale Institute.

A member of the US Olympic sheet shooting team in the 1968 Olympics, Bob took an interest in bicycle racing at the games that would lead to building a velodrome in Trexlertown in 1974.

Bob Rodale joined forces with the Wildlands Conservancy in 1976 in acquiring land for preserving open space. He donated 92 acres of land in the South Mountain area near Emmaus for preservation in 1978.

In 1975, Rodale added a new 37,600-square-foot distribution facility at 400 South 10th Street.

During Rodale's expansion, instead of demolishing a home now known as the 1803 House that sat on part of Rodale's property, Bob partitioned the property and after discussions with Council, presented the deed to the Borough. Ardath Rodale, Bob's wife, along with friend and community activist Elsie Yarema, took on the task of restoring the house. The Friends of the 1803 House was formed to maintain and preserve the house. It is now listed in the National Register of Historic Places and serves as a museum for the community to view life in the 1800s.

In 1985, Rodale built a 10,000 square foot facility for fitness and wellness classes for Rodale employees known as the Energy Center. The company also purchased the Thaddeus Stevens Elementary School and regenerated it as the Rodale Food Center.

Both Bob and Ardie continued to contribute, both as volunteers and financially, to institutions and events in the Emmaus area.

On September 20, 1990, Bob was tragically killed in a traffic accident while on a business trip in Russia. Upon Bob's death, Ardie became the company's Chief Executive Officer (CEO) and Chairman of the Board.

In 2000, when a group of Emmaus residents, led by Dr. Michael Waddell, began a memorial park project designed to honor Emmaus residents with commemorative bricks and plaques, Ardie was happy to help, contributing funds for the construction of a pergola at the Knauss Homestead site of the park.

Rodale added a child care center in 2001 at 420 South 10th Street.

Rodale supported the creation of the Rodale Aquatic Center at Cedar Crest College with a donation of $1 million dollars. Its dedication was in 2002.

You can't go far in Emmaus without touching an area or organization that hasn't been fostered in some way by the company and by Bob and Ardie Rodale. The Rodale Family Foundation continues the family's philanthropic legacy, recently funding the resurfacing of the Emmaus High School Track, among other projects.

As the 2009 anniversary year came to a close, Ardie Rodale passed away at the age of 81. Emmaus architect and historian Alan Hawman said upon hearing of Ardie's death, "She was part of the past, a path to the present, and will be remembered in the future." Maria Rodale too over as CEO and Chariman of the Board in September 2009.

Robin Kertis contributed to this article
Source: *Our Roots Grow Deep*, Rodale, 2008.

Moravian Church 2009

Former Businesses . . .

Craumer's Variety 5 & 10 Cent Store

After the Great Depression, Marvin Craumer and his wife, Anne, decided to open a 5 & 10 Cent Store, an ideal choice for those hard times. After studying maps and locations, they decided that Emmaus was the biggest town in the area without one. They found a location at Sixth and Chestnut Streets, where they sold notions, stationery, candies and cookies, basic hardware, and housewares.

As sales improved and their inventory became more valuable, they needed more space. Mr. Craumer made a deal with Arthur P. Hauser to rent the best spot in town, on the Triangle at Fourth and Chestnut Streets. He connected with the best sources for "variety stores." To further increase his buying power for seasonal merchandise, he joined forces with Mr. Dotterer in Boyertown and Mr. Smith in Kutztown, who had similar stores.

In the early 1950s, the Acme store across the street closed and Mr. Craumer bought the building and opened the Triangle Shop—a women's dress shop run by Arlene Dennis and Grace Treichler. Around this time, Robert Guinther bought the variety store so that Mr. Craumer could concentrate his efforts on the Triangle Shop.

48

Joe Semancik's Hobby Shop

A business located at 412 Chestnut Street was purchased from Willard Doney in 1970. It was mainly an electrical shop with hobbies as a sideline. Joe Semancik operated the business strictly as a hobby shop at the Chestnut Street location for several years before moving to 8 S. 4th Street on the Triangle. The shop became a well-known spot for the youth and adults of the Emmaus community to learn and develop their hobby skills and model railroad interests.

Emmaus Pharmacy

The Emmaus Pharmacy opened in 1962 and closed in 1972. The store had an old-fashioned soda fountain that served food and ice cream sundaes. John J. Swift, the owner, loved his store and providing a service to the community. He had a car that had pills drawn all over it that he used to deliver prescriptions to those who could not drive or who were ill.

The pharmacy became a community center for local folks who came in for a good joke or company. Mr. Swift was passionate about his customers and in caring for them. He used to say that he saved many a life by alerting doctors to prescription combinations that could be harmful. He made prescription recipes, now called "compounding," which is how he learned pharmacy.

Rodale Manufacturing Co., Inc

The Rodale Manufacturing Co. began in 1930 in New York City when Joseph (Joe) Rodale left his employment as a salesman to manufacture the products he had been selling. He noted the advantage and pace of living in a small town and chose to relocate his factory to a small two-story building at 6th and Minor Streets in Emmaus.

Joined by his brother, J. I. Rodale, the company grew rapidly, at its height employing more than four hundred people. It manufactured household items such as toggle switches, duplex receptacles, cord connectors, extension cords, and so on. He employed only local residents and became the major support for many families. In the 1930s, the company prospered in the small two-story building and expanded to three stories. When World War II prevented the company from obtaining materials for his products, Rodale was soon manufacturing gun mounts for US Navy ships.

Joe Rodale was a leading figure in Emmaus and Allentown in the 30s, 40s, and very early 50s. He was a founding member of the Emmaus Lion's Club, spearheading the drive for Emmaus to have its own ambulance corps.

He served as president of the Boots and Saddle Riding Club. He fulfilled a dream in the Rodale Arabian Stud Farm, where he bred purebred Arabians. He built the farm on Fish Hatchery Road and raised all the feed for the horses. The farm became a major tourist attraction in eastern Pennsylvania. Joe died in 1952 at the age of fifty-six.

{ **49**

Platt Fur Company

Henry Platt owned and operated the Platt Fur Company in Emmaus from 1939 until 1964. The business began in the basement of his home, but during most of those years it was located on the Triangle, at 12-14 South Fourth Street, in a building then owned by the Emaus Telephone Company. After the Emmaus business closed, he continued to manufacture fur garments for another two decades in Allentown under the name of Henry Platt Furs.

Platt Fur Company sold fur coats, jackets, and stoles at retail and manufactured them for sale throughout the United States. Through the retail establishment, the company sold new and custom-made furs, as well as repaired, remodeled, and stored fur garments. At its peak, the company employed twenty people and manufactured more than 10,000 fur garments a year. The company produced everything from the finest mink coats to children's bunny furs. Mr. Platt also made novelty fur items such as Davy Crockett hats and fur bow (beaux) ties through his Kenwell Fur Novelty Company. He developed a process to curl sheared rabbit fur to create faux Persian lamb skins and also was recognized in the trade for his innovative streamlining of many of the processes used to manufacture fur garments.

In the front of the manufacturing side of the business, Mr. Platt maintained a community display window, which he made available without cost to Scout, school, and other nonprofit organizations to publicize their events, celebrations, and programs.

Dundore's Drug Store

Harry W. Dundore was born on November 13, 1879, in Bernville, Berks County, Pennsylvania, to Madon and Mary Dundore. After 8th grade, he became a teacher to put himself through the Philadelphia School of Pharmacy and Science.

He married Laura Jones and they came to Emmaus. He worked as a pharmacist for Mr. Stonebach, whose drugstore was in the Old Bank Building on S. 4th Street Harry and Laura had two children, Roy and Ruth. After college Roy joined his father as a pharmacist.

In 1937, Harry had A. P. Houser build 8-10 S. 4th Street No.10 was the pharmacy and soda fountain. After Harry's death in 1943, Roy continued the business at No.10 until his death in 1969, when the pharmacy was sold to Lester Harwick. Later, No.10 would become a pinball space, the office of *The Free Press*, and then a pet store. No.8 was an office, then a luncheonette, and later a retail space. The building remained in the Dundore family until 1994, when it was sold to Eugene Schantzenbach.

Weida's Luncheonette

In 1945, the Weida brothers, Donald, Amos, and Wayne, opened their first Luncheonette and Bakery in Quakertown. In 1947, they heard that Roy Dundore in Emmaus was considering dividing his drugstore and renting out 8 South 4th Street. The brothers decided to open another luncheonette. The rent was to be $150.00 a month.

Arlene Polster maintained the kitchen. Her homemade baked beans, potato salad, and assorted other salads and spreads, along with fresh orangeade, lemonade, ice cream sodas, sundaes, hot dogs, and hamburgers helped make the luncheonette a success.

In 1952, when parking meters were installed around the Triangle and Main Street, the brothers decided to look for property where they would have more parking for a food business. They sold the Quakertown and Emmaus luncheonettes and opened the Charcoal Drive-In in Wescosville in 1953.

Schuster Hex Signs & Gift Shop

William and Charlotte Schuster moved from Vera Cruz to 423 Chestnut Street in Emmaus in 1952. The Schusters enclosed the front porch so that they had two rooms full of gifts and hex signs. William painted and lettered in the low ceiling basement until he had the barn in the backyard torn down to build a workshop. The gift shop sold ceramics, clocks, glass, Westmoreland milk glass, candy dishes, and so on.

After selling the property in 1992, he moved the business to Kutztown. The Schusters have been making hex signs for fifty-four years including their time in the present shop in Kutztown from which he sells most of his stock at the Kutztown Folk Festival.

Roberts Coal and Supply Company

The Roberts family bought a coal yard in 1928 at the corner of 6th and Chestnut Streets in Emmaus. Christine Roberts operated the business for close to thirty years. She retired and sold the property to the Merritt Lumber Company, which bought the property because it wanted the railroad siding for lumber deliveries.

The property extended from Chestnut Street back to the railroad tracks, where a siding allowed the locomotives to receive coal deliveries. The office building at the corner was quite small. At some point she ceased to have the coal delivered by rail and had it trucked in from the mine. Just outside the small building on the south side, under the limbs of a tree, was a large boulder of coal, which always fascinated the children. Also on the south side of the property was a gas station that she owned and rented.

Mrs. Roberts was a shrewd businesswoman, but she was also kind and caring. She was well liked in the Emaus community and was involved in many civic affairs. According to her daughter, Christine Roberts Fraley, "one bitter cold winter day during the depression when three ragged children came to the door of the office pulling an express wagon, the oldest boy held out his hand with fifty cents in it and said to my mother, 'We are so cold at home. This is all the money our dad had. Would you give us that much coal so that we can be warm for a little bit?' Mother took the fifty cents and instructed Gene, the driver, to fill as many burlap bags with coal as the wagon would hold."

{ **51**

Terry's Restaurant

Terry and Gail Prutsman opened Terry's Steak Shop at 515 Chestnut Street in Emmaus on April 1, 1967. In the beginning, it was open only for lunch and dinner. They later added breakfast, at which time they changed the name to Terry's Family Restaurant.

Terry and his family enjoyed every patron as a friend. After Terry passed away in 1982, the family kept the restaurant operating until September 1994. Since the doors have closed, many past patrons have come to the family to tell them how much they miss the great food and atmosphere of Terry's. Indeed, these were some of the best years of the Prutsman family's lives. The family wishes to thank all of their loyal patrons/friends for the wonderful memories.

Professional Organizations

Business & Professional Women of Emmaus

Business & Professional Women of Emmaus was organized on March 10, 1947. The Emmaus chapter name BPW/Emmaus was changed on November 15, 1999, to reflect the local membership, which encompasses the Lehigh Valley area. Today, BPW/Emmaus is known as BPW/Lehigh Valley.

BPW was one of the first women's organizations to formally endorse the Equal Rights Amendment in 1937, and they have led the drive for ratification ever since. BPW/PA has endorsed many financial projects, including purchase of cancer research equipment, victims flood relief, and scholarships and interest-free grants to members. It supports programs that will advance the cause of working women.

Every October, BPW/Lehigh Valley actively participates in National Business Women's Week by celebrating the accomplishments of workingwomen and awarding a Niki to an outstanding local working woman. They also recognize local women veterans through their National Women Joining Forces coalition.

Women's History Month is celebrated in March by partnering with the East Penn School District and sponsoring a bookmark contest. Locally, they have supported Turning Point and other local agencies. Through the state federation they have partnered with the American Heart Association and the Susan G. Komen Foundation.

{ 53

East Penn Chamber of Commerce

The East Penn Chamber of Commerce traces its roots to the Emmaus Chamber of Commerce. According to the Borough of Emmaus Centennial Celebration Official Souvenir Program published in 1959, the Emmaus Chamber of Commerce was founded in 1937 to:

- Develop, encourage, promote and protect the commercial, professional, financial and general business interests of the Borough of Emmaus

- Promote the civic interests and general welfare of the community

- Encourage the development of transportation and communication facilities and the various resources of the borough

- Procure laws and regulations desirable to the benefit of business in general and provide for a forum for the reflection of sentiments of business regarding matters affecting its interests.

In the late 1990s, the Emmaus Chamber of Commerce joined with what was then known as the Allentown Chamber of Commerce to become the first Regional Council of the Lehigh County Chamber of Commerce.

Today the chamber is known as the Greater Lehigh Valley Chamber of Commerce and is the second largest in Pennsylvania. The East Penn Business Council widened its geographic scope to include all municipalities that comprise the East Penn School District. The Council is comprised of fifteen elected members.

In 2009, the objectives of the Council are to:

- Identify opportunities for intergovernmental and community cooperation and provide specific recommendations to the five East Penn municipalities and Lehigh County

- Facilitate economic development efforts across the East Penn community and continue to provide assistance to established downtown programs

- Facilitate and enhance the development and modernization of infrastructure to improve the quality of life in the region.

Council leaders in 2008/2009 are President John Hayes, president of Great Bear Bank; Vice-President Joseph Farkas, Aspire Consulting; 2nd Vice President Kevin Baker, Air Products; Past President Francee Fuller, Barry Isett & Associates.

Emmaus Commemorative Gardens Foundation (ECGF)

The Emmaus Commemorative Gardens Foundation (ECGF) began in 2002 as a Task Force Team of the Emmaus Visioning Project. The initial project team used a memorial rose garden in Hawthorne, Nevada as the inspiration for the garden but redesigned the concept to fit the Knauss Homestead site with a Moravianesque style. Called The Remembrance Garden at the Knauss Homestead, the foundation wanted to create a rose garden that honors the Moravian culture and serves as a contemporary space for reflection. The quarter-acre garden is a meeting place where generations of current and future Emmaus residents can share memories of the past and plans for the future.

The ECGF is a volunteer organization dedicated to creating special commemorative garden sites in Emmaus. The ECGF directs the development of the current garden site at the Knauss Homestead. Presentations about the project have been made to a wide range of local organizations to educate the public and to encourage people and groups to purchase commemoratives, including bricks, roses, benches, trees, and perennials.

The site was dedicated in July 2004 with the installation of the first bricks. To date there have been more than 150 bricks installed for families, service club members, high school students, businesses, friends, and veterans.

The Emmaus Arts Commission

In 1985, the Borough of Emmaus established the Emmaus Arts Commission to support the arts on a public level. Though dormant until 2005, today the Emmaus Arts Commission is the premier arts organization in Emmaus. Its mission is to encourage and promote all of the arts and to develop an appreciation of the arts, which will enrich and enhance the quality of life in Emmaus and its environs.

With the backing of the Emmaus Borough Council and surrounding businesses, the Emmaus Arts Commission focuses on the delivery of the arts, such as fine art, music, craft, dance, and theatre to the general public. Its events, such as Art in the Garden, the Emmaus Art Walk, the Student Horror Film Festival, and SnowBlast Winter Festival have become quite popular. The Emmaus Arts Commission encourages and stimulates public interest and participation in the cultural heritage of our region. The Commission supports the growth, development, and preservation of the arts within Emmaus and the Lehigh Valley.

Emmaus Flag Day Association

The Emmaus Flag Day Association (EFDA) was founded in 1969, during the height of the Vietnam War, as a response to flag burning associated with some antiwar protests at that time. The original purpose of the organization was to imbue respect for the nation's flag through programs in the community, especially in the schools.

In 1970, the Boy Scouts of America local troop leaders in the Borough held an essay contest based on the statement: "What the American Flag Means to Me." The winning entries were read at Emmaus Community Park that year for the Flag Day program. In 1976, an essay program was offered to all the East Penn and parochial elementary schools. In 1977, Mrs. Susan Koltisko, a teacher in the East Penn Junior High School, took over the essay program and added a poetry contest. Susan oversaw the essay and poetry contest until 2006 at which time Marjory Heatley became president.

Four veterans' organizations—Veterans Committee, Catholic War Vets, American Legion, and VFW—partner with the EFDA, each contributing $100 yearly toward the expenses of the contest and banquet.

The essay contest is now for eighth graders, while the poetry contest is restricted to fifth graders, with virtually all teachers in these grades participating. Six winners are awarded a trophy plus a flag and certificate from their state representative at an annual banquet held at the Moravian Church. At the Community Park Flag Day Program, where they read their entry to the public, student participants receive a flag set and certificate from our state senator.

Besides the annual contest, the EFDA provides flags for the Triangle, which the Borough installs, as well as flags on 4th St Bridge on special holidays and sells and installs flag sets for businesses and homes in the community.

{ 55

Emmaus Lions Club

The Emmaus Lions Club was founded in 1945 when a group of men felt a need for a service organization in the Emmaus area. Since then, the Emmaus Lions Club has distributed more than one million dollars to the needy and visually impaired in the community.

Among the many projects/organizations the club supports are eye exams, eyeglasses, and hearing aids for the needy; a drug and alcohol awareness program; the Emmaus Ambulance Corps; Emmaus fire companies; the Shelter House; the Emmaus Public Library; community ball fields and playgrounds; and the Emmaus Police Department Drug and Protection K-9 program.

Emmaus Lioness Club

The Emmaus Lioness Club was formed on October 8, 1979, and chartered on March 22, 1980, with a membership of fifty-four women. Lionism's primary function is to provide community and charitable outreach to those less fortunate and those in need of love, understanding, and assistance. Lionism is not a club but a way of life. Through service to others there is enlightenment and growth.

Some of their past and present projects are recipe books, homemade comforters, a quilt, pot-pie supper, Build Your Own Scarecrow Project, Creative Basket Party, Apple Dumplings, Lioness Golf Tournament, and My Father's Wallet (helping needy school children). They are proud to be involved in helping the blind community through Beacon Lodge Camp, Northeast Eye Bank, Leader Dogs for the Blind, sight conservation and eye research, as well as their local Lehigh Valley County Association for the Blind and Visually Impaired.

Local community contributions include the ambulance and fire departments, Emmaus Public Library, Memorial Gardens honoring our presidents, various projects at Emmaus Community Park, as well as a yearly scholarship to a student who enters the physical therapy or education field.

Emmaus Farmers' Market

The Friends of the Emmaus Farmers' Market took form at a break-out session of the Emmaus Visioning Project. In 2003, the market opened with the Emmaus Main Street Program (EMSP) serving as administrator, treasurer, and on-site manager. After two years, an Emmaus Farmers' Market Board of Directors was formed and by-laws written and adopted. With much pride in the market's success, the EMSP turned the market over to the newly developed group and the Emmaus Farmers' Market grew to what we know today.

The market is in its seventh season with twenty producers, offering a wide variety of local and seasonal produce and products, including many types of fruits

emmaus
HOMEGROWN
farmers'
market
www.emmausmarket.com

and vegetables as well as bison, chicken, goats' milk cheeses, pastries, pies, breads, and flowers. The market is more than just a place to buy local high-quality, organic produce; it is also a place to meet friends, neighbors, and family. Each Sunday shoppers are treated to the sounds of live music and have the opportunity to stop at one of our local community booths to get information, sign up as a volunteer, or offer other kinds of support. The mission of the market is to provide the Emmaus community with a source of safe, locally produced, highly nutritious produce while educating the public, including farmers, on the benefits of supporting local agriculture in order to preserve farmland in the surrounding area, improve individual health, and strengthen community.

Emmaus Garden Club

A WPA Project class on Gardening and Nature Lore was taught in 1935 at Emmaus High School by Miss Doris Benson. After two months, the class ended because Miss Benson could not devote the required number of hours for a WPA project, but the twenty participants became the Garden Club in 1938. Their "Borough Beautiful" motto in 1938 gave rise to the adoption of the forsythia as the official borough flower in 1941. By this time there were fifty-seven Club members. By the 10th anniversary, there were ninety members, and in January, 1949, one hundred ninety one members were reported. The Emmaus Garden Club was admitted to the Federation of Garden Clubs in 1949.

The Garden Club has offered many programs and activities to members and has sponsored many community activities. A yearly chrysanthemum exhibit at the American Legion Hall drew sizeable crowds. Spring flower shows became a yearly event along with trips to Longwood Gardens and the Philadelphia Flower Show. Planting tulips and flowers at the Triangle and around the town, contributing to the community food bank, participating in community special events, funding scholarships for students furthering their studies in plant-related fields, and going into the schools with conservation and Arbor Day programs were cherished activites.

From the beginning, many community-minded people have guided the Emmaus Garden Club, including, most recently, Elaine Klase, Jackie Todaro, Dr. Mary Horkowitz, Sandi Miklos, Dorothy Nicholas, Sandra Bachman, Rose Parry, and for many dedicated years, Frank and Lucie Laudenslager. The "Borough Beautiful" motto endures.

The Emmaus Rotary Club

Rotary began in Chicago in 1905 when several businessmen thought it might be useful to meet periodically to socialize and promote their respective businesses. It was decided the meetings should rotate among the group to better facilitate their meetings. Thus began Rotary, which, by the mid-1920s, had grown rapidly, spreading not only to most parts of the country but in many other places in the world as well.

In the fall of 1925, Earl Peters, an Allentown music teacher then living in Emaus and a member of the Allentown Rotary Club, suggested to some Emmaus friends that they start a club. On December 16, 1925, several Emmaus businessmen and professionals met to organize the club. The Emmaus Charter (No. 2251) was signed by R.I. President Donald A. Adams on February 22, 1926, and the initial meeting of the Club took place on March 18, 1926.

Over its eight-four-year history, the Emmaus Rotary Club has met in many different places, including the Grange Hall in Macungie, Broad Street Saloon, Pine Tree Tavern, Fire Company No. 2, Mercantile Club, Marcel's, the Superior Diner, and, most recently, Brookside Country Club. Special meetings have been held in such places as the ABE Airport, Willow Grove Naval Air Station, Dorney Park, Queen City Airport, Good Shepherd Home, and the Lehigh Valley Dairy. Membership has fluctuated from its original twenty-two to a post-Second World War high of seventy-six in 1953 to a low of twenty-eight in the early 1990s. Its current membership is at an all-time high with ninety-eight in 2009.

Since its founding, Rotary has become one of the pre-eminent philanthropic organizations in the world, reflecting its mission of promoting international peace through good works and cultural understanding. Over the past sixty years alone, its members have contributed more than one billion dollars to various causes, the most famous of which is its leadership in eliminating polio throughout the world. The Emmaus Club has reflected this culture of community outreach, contributing to a wide variety of groups such as scouting programs, the Emmaus Public Library, Community Park, the fire companies, and the schools. Specifically, it spearheaded the construction of the Arts Pavilion in Community Park, provided computers and landscaping for the library, and contributed the kiosk for the guest center at the Pool Wildlife Sanctuary, a playground at the Community Park, a gazebo outside the Lower Macungie Township Library, and, most recently, the kiosk at the new Triangle Park in Emmaus. Internationally, it raised money for a cancer research center in rural India, housing for the homeless in Brazil, the renovation of the science labs at Warren East High School in New Orleans, and tsunami relief in Sri Lanka.

The Emmaus Rotary Club has been an important part of the Greater Western Lehigh Valley area for over three-quarters of a century and hopes to remain so for many years to come. It is proud of its Emmaus roots and its role in promoting one of the Top 100 Small Towns in America.

Emmaus Senior Citizen Club

The Emmaus Senior Citizen Club was organized in 1953, meeting at the Moravian Church Fellowship Hall. It is the second oldest senior citizen organization in Lehigh County. The group met in various locations through the years and now meets at St. Matthew's E.C. at Fifth and Ridge Streets in Emmaus. Average attendance is between fifty and sixty members.

Except for the months of July and August, its weekly meetings are every Friday at 1 pm (doors open earlier for those who want to come and kibitz). Coffee and a snack are served and usually there is a program consisting of a speaker or entertainer. If not, then a movie is shown, except for the last Friday of every month, which is game day for Bingo or other card games. Occasional bus trips, a picnic in June, and a Christmas banquet in December are highlights of the year.

A donation of $1.25 is paid at each meeting, which covers the refreshments plus entertainment. Anyone fifty-five years or older is welcome to join in for friendship and fun.

The Emmaus Sentinels Drum and Bugle Corps

The Emmaus Sentinels Drum and Bugle Corps was founded in 1924 as the American Legion Drill Team at the Henry Schaefer Post No. 191. It was comprised of men returning from World War I. The Legion Drum and Bugle Corps was founded in 1930. Donning uniforms of maroon wool coats, tan knickers, black boots, and chrome dome hats, they marched in any parade in the Lehigh Valley and nearby communities.

In 1962, the Corps took the field in competition and changed its name to the Emmaus Sentinels. Sponsorship remained with the American Legion and it became a part of the Red Carpet Association (RCA). In 1967, it won the Senior Division in competition and continued on to win the American Legion State Championships that year. It participated in Emmaus' Bicentennial Parade in 1976. With the decline of RCA corps, they were unable to field a corps for the 1976-1977 season and discontinued operation.

Under the leadership of Tracy Dell and Brad Fogel, the Corps was resurrected and started practicing in 2007 for the 2009 Anniversary Celebration Parade. With financial support from the Borough, the Emmaus General Authority, and private citizens, the Corps plans to continue into the future.

Environmental Advisory Council

"Fostering the protection and enhancement of our local and regional natural resources"

The Environmental Advisory Council (EAC) was jointly formed by the Borough of Emmaus and Upper Milford Township in January 2005. Comprised of eight members—four individuals appointed from each community—the EAC's mission is to advise elected officials, local planning commissions, parks and recreation boards, as well as the public, in matters regarding the conservation, management, and protection of natural resources within the two communities. The council works to identify environmental problems, issues, and trends affecting both municipalities and fostering cooperation between the regulatory boards and the public in making environmentally sound decisions. Areas of special interest to the EAC include:

- Protecting and preserving local and regional water resources
- Restoration and protection of the Leibert Creek Watershed
- Recycling and waste management
- Storm water management
- Land use
- Open space preservation

The EAC holds an annual Earth Day cleanup event, which has grown every year since its inception. In 2008, the event hosted about one hundred forty volunteers who picked up two hundred fifty bags of garbage from sites around the borough and in the township, while 2009's event attracted more than 300 participants. Another education project the EAC initiated is a storm-drain stenciling program to inform residents that materials dumped down the borough's storm drains flow directly to our waterways.

GFWC PA Woman's Club of Emmaus

The Woman's Club of Emmaus was organized in February, 1940 with one hundred thirty-four members. In 1941, the first graduation prize was awarded. In 1948, the first scholarship and sports award were given. The Girl-of-the-Month Awards began in 1953. Harpster Memorial Awards began in 1991. All continue to the present date.

Since 1943, the Club has supported the Emmaus Public Library with money and volunteer hours. Its Community Welfare Committee donates food baskets or certificates to needy families at the holidays. The first Youth Center Dances were held in 1944 and continued for twenty-five years. In 1946, the Daughter's Division was organized, the Newcomers Club in 1949, and the Junior Woman's Club in 1951. In 1953, the Woman's Club sponsored the Senior Citizen Club, serving seniors every Friday for thirty years.

In 1959, two of their yearbooks were placed in the Time Capsule. The club cookbook, *What's Cookin?* was published in 1962—the first such cookbook in the area made up of members' recipes. In 1978, the tradition of planting a tree on Arbor Day to honor club presidents was begun. This tradition is still being honored. A Memorial Picnic Pavilion was constructed at Community Park and dedicated in 1983 to the cause of peace. It has donated money for the preservation of the Shelter House and the 1803 House as well as for local, county, state, and general federal projects.

Soroptimist International

Begun in 1921, Soroptimist International, which by 2009 was operating in more than one hundred countries, is the largest classified service organization for women. Its members are dedicated to providing community service on the local, national, and worldwide levels. "Soro" means sister, and "optima" means best, making the name Soroptimist connote the best of and for women.

Soroptimist International of Emmaus was established in 1958 and has worked to provide education awards for deserving women and citizenship awards and scholarships for high school students. Organizations such as the Emmaus Ambulance Corps, Emmaus Library, Jenn's House, Turning Point, and local food banks have also benefited, as well as local needy families.

Soroptimists also reach out to countries far and wide, giving aid following natural and man-made disasters, and providing help to women in difficult situations beyond their control.

Emmaus Kiwanis Club

The Emmaus Kiwanis Club, which was organized on December 30, 1951, has been an active and vital part of the community since its founding.

The Kiwanis Club of Emmaus looks outward as well as inward. It reaches out to attract members from the greater Emmaus and East Penn community. It offers its members personal growth through hearty fellowship and teamwork and encourages the formation of strong friendships. Club membership includes men and women in a wide range of occupations.

Some of the activities and programs the club sponsors are Emmaus High School and Whitehall High School Key Clubs, Lower Macungie and Eyer Middle Schools Builders Clubs, several boy's and girl's sports teams, the annual Easter Egg Hunt in Community Park, the Walter C. Stoudt Memorial Prayer Breakfast, and an annual Christmas party for the mentally handicapped.

Churches of Emmaus

Bethel Bible Fellowship Church

418 Elm Street

Christ! Passion! People!

In 1882, Rev. Jonas Musselman moved to Emmaus and, urged by members and friends in the area, held evangelistic services in Emmaus in what was then known as Wieand's Church on Chestnut Street. The services led to the organization of the congregation and the purchase of a two-story frame building at 431 Chestnut Street. They remained at that site for more than fifty years, until January 1933, when they moved to their current 418 Elm Street church. As the congregation continued to grow, expansions were added in 1967 and 1988.

God did amazing things with the Bethel Church leadership's commitment to stay in Emmaus. With that faith, God allowed all five adjacent North Street properties to be purchased in just over three years. The church's journey to keep up with what God has been doing continued into 2008 with the dedication of a large multipurpose room/gymnasium with additional classrooms. The Finale for the 2009 Celebration was held in this new gym with a stage and kitchen providing exceptional accommodations for a crowd of three hundred.

St. Ann's Roman Catholic Church

415 S. 6th Street

The history of Saint Ann Parish began in 1763 when Father Schneider, a Jesuit missionary, celebrated a marriage in Macunshi [Macungie], which is now part of Saint Ann Parish. Throughout the nineteenth century, the spiritual needs of the local Catholic population were met by traveling missionaries. As the immigrant population began to rise at the turn of the twentieth century, a priest from Saint John the Baptist Slovak Catholic Church in Allentown visited Emmaus and celebrated Mass the third Sunday of every month in a private home.

By 1921, Mass was being celebrated in the second floor hall of a general store on Minor Street, and thirteen acres of farmland were purchased as the site for the future Saint Ann's Catholic Church. The cornerstone was laid on Thanksgiving Day, 1923.

{ 63

Construction began in 1928 and was completed in May 1929. Rev. Paul M. Pekarik was appointed the first pastor of Saint Ann's in 1930. The rectory was constructed in 1938.

The school began in 1949 with one hundred thirty two students in classrooms constructed in the church basement. In 1954, Saint Ann School's first building was opened with an enrollment of two hundred seventy three students. In 1957, a gym and extra classrooms were added.

The congregation outgrew the old church and the present church was constructed in 1982 during the administration of the second pastor, the Rev. James E. Sweeney. In 1997, during the pastorate of the Rev. Msgr. Thomas E. Hoban, an addition to the school with offices, science lab, library, computer lab, plus kindergarten and pre-school classrooms was dedicated. In 2004, another addition with art and music rooms and more classrooms was added. Msgr. Hoban retired in 2008, and the Rev. Msgr. John S. Mraz was named the fourth pastor of Saint Ann's.

St. John's Lutheran Church
Fifth & Chestnut Streets

In 1742, the first Lutherans in the area that would become Emmaus met to worship in a little log church at what is now Third and Adrian Streets. When Emmaus became exclusively Moravian a few years later, Lutherans did not worship again in Emmaus until 1875. The Lutheran and Reformed people in Emmaus began worshipping (on alternate Sundays) in the Moravian Church in 1875 and formally organized in 1882 when they built the Union Church, which still stands at the corner of North Third and Green Streets. 1882 is considered the official year of the founding of St. John's Lutheran Church. The organizer of the Lutheran congregation was the Rev. William Rath, the pastor of the Western Salisbury Lutheran congregation, which shared its pastor with St. John's until 1944.

In 1922, the union relationship (a Lutheran and a Reformed congregation sharing a single building) dissolved. The Lutheran congregation dedicated its new building at Fifth and Chestnut Streets in October 1924. In 1954, the Parish Education building was added to the original church building. In 1983, major renovations were made to the sanctuary. In 2007, major restoration work was done on the bell tower.

In its 127-year history, St. John's has been served by eight pastors, three of whom served notably long tenures: the Rev. Myron O. Rath (1890–1920), the Rev. Paul F. Spieker (1928–1960), and the Rev. Fred S. Foerster (1970–2001). The Rev. Wayne A. Matthias-Long has been pastor since 2002. St. John's ministries emphasize service to the community and the world. They welcome all people to join them in "putting on the working clothes of the gospel" to do God's work with our hands.

St. John's United Church of Christ
139 North Street

In January 1876, approximately sixty people of the Reformed tradition organized a Reformed congregation in Emmaus. The young congregations of the Reformed and Lutheran traditions consecrated a union in early 1882.

The two congregations dedicated their new church building, located at the corner of North Third Street and Green Alley, on November 12, 1882. The united congregations worshipped there for thirty-eight years until building a new large gothic structure at the corner of North Fourth and North Streets. Dedication of the new building was on May 4, 1924.

In June 1934, the Reformed Church merged with the Evangelical Synod of North America, forming the Evangelical and Reformed Church. Then, in June 1957, another merger took place with the Congregational Christian Churches forming the United Church of Christ. The Christian Education wing was dedicated in 1963. Many outstanding pastors have served the church. The current pastor is Rev. Paul W. Knappenberger.

Lehigh Valley Baptist Church
4702 Colebrook Avenue, Upper Milford

The Lehigh Valley Baptist Church began with ten people in November 1977, holding weekly Bible studies in Timothy Buck's home. The first Sunday service was January 15, 1978, in a rented church building in Emmaus with thirty attendees. In ten months, the church outgrew the building and moved to the Swain School. The church purchased its present 14.44-acre site in Emmaus on November 2, 1979, including a stone 19th century barn and farmhouse. Services began in their newly renovated home in September, 1980.

A two-story educational wing was added in 1982 for a Christian school, grades K-12. In the years following, other buildings were added on the property for church and school staff. On January 1, 1988, Pastor Douglas Hammett moved to the Lehigh Valley to meet the challenge of continuing the forward movement of the Lehigh Valley Baptist Church.

In March 1991, a special Dedication Service was held for the 10,000-square-foot facility that housed a six-hundred-seat auditorium. This new addition also includes the Book Heaven Bible Bookstore, which provides Christian books and bibles for the congregation and the public, and the Lehigh Valley Baptist Bible Institute, which provides men with instruction for pastoral and missionary training.

The Lutheran Church of the Holy Spirit
3461 Cedar Crest Boulevard

The congregation of the Lutheran Church of the Holy Spirit began with a meeting of a small group of Lutherans on July 3, 1960. During that summer they provided Sunday School in six of their homes and worshiped in various local churches. Forty families held their first worship service in November 1960 at 184 Jefferson Street, Emmaus. The official organization of the church in May 1961 listed a roll of seventy-five confirmed members. The church's first building on Cedar Crest Boulevard next to Emmaus High School was dedicated in June 1965. As the congregation flourished, educational units, offices, and a larger sanctuary were added.

Today, with a congregation of more than twelve hundred, the church provides three Sunday services, traditional and contemporary, with music being an important part of the proceedings. Sunday School is held for all—children through adults. An exciting new worship service "Rejoicing Spirits," geared to and led by disabled persons, but welcoming to all, is held the second Sunday of every month. The building is alive through the week with nursery school, choirs, seniors, support, study, and interest groups. Throughout the year, more than thirty community groups use the facilities.

Holy Spirit was begun as a witness to our faith and a strong commitment to ministry in daily life and continues to welcome people to join to become more faithful disciples of Jesus Christ in our homes, our communities, and the world.

St. Margaret's Episcopal Church
Elm & Keystone

St. Margaret's Episcopal Church, Keystone and Elm Streets, celebrated its 100th Anniversary in 2008. Its years are marked by service to the community and growth in faith and numbers of members. The family and friends of Emmanuel Derr first met in a rented store on Main Street, enduring the cold, drafts, and a leaky roof.

The congregation grew and built a church on Fourth and Broad Streets in the 1930s. Young men training for the ministry at Leonard Hall in Fountain Hill conducted their first services there until 1957 when the current building on Elm and Keystone Streets was dedicated. Since then, there have been two additions, with rooms for Christian education, a chapel, and a parish office. Parish life centers around the Sunday celebrations of Holy Eucharist. Each November, the parish celebrates its heritage on St. Margaret's Day with bagpipes, special dress, and a luncheon. (Margaret, queen of Scotland, encouraged the building of schools, hospitals, and orphanages.)

St. Margaret's understands itself to be a "small but mighty" church. In January 2010, the parish plans to start a Family School where adults will be tutored one evening a week while their children are watched. The St. Margaret's Nursery School, founded in 1981, continues to welcome children. In March 2001, a team traveled to Honduras to help rebuild after Hurricane Mitch; St. Margaret's worked to settle a refugee family from Liberia here in the Lehigh Valley five years ago. The Rev. Canon Lexa H. Shallcross is the current Rector.

St. Paul's Orthodox Christian Church
156 East Main

St. Paul's Antiochian Orthodox Christian Church, a parish of the 2,000-year-old Orthodox Church of Antioch, was founded in Emmaus in 1987. A mission of St. George Orthodox Church in Allentown, St. Paul's began its life worshipping in a tiny church building on S. 4th Street near the Emmaus Triangle, under the leadership of Emmaus native Fr. John Kahle, its founding pastor. In 1997, the congregation, having grown significantly, moved to its present location at 156 E. Main Street next to the Cintas building.

In 1999, Fr. John retired, and he was succeeded by the newly ordained Fr. Theodore Mikovich, a retired public school teacher who had been serving as the parish deacon for two years. Fr. Theodore served the parish as pastor for the next ten years. In 2003, Thomas Underwood, an Easton firefighter and sheriff's deputy, was ordained to serve the parish as deacon. In 2009, Fr. Theodore retired, and Fr. Andrew S. Damick was appointed as pastor, having served for two years previously as assistant pastor at the Orthodox cathedral in Charleston, West Virginia.

Today, St. Paul's is home to a diverse collection of families and believers, representing multiple backgrounds and religious histories. Worship services according to the ancient Orthodox Christian tradition are held in English daily.

{ **67**

West Valley Presbyterian Church of America
326 Main Street, Suite 1

In March 2008, thirty adults and their children gathered in Mas Café to prayerfully discuss planting a church in the growing "West Valley" (Emmaus, Macungie, Lower Macungie). The gathering was a product of the vision of Cornerstone Presbyterian Church (Coopersburg). Little did they know that the first year of worship services would be on Main Street, in the renovated Clock building (beginning September 2008). They thank God for pitching their tent in Emmaus, a borough with a contagious culture of art, history, creativity, and community.

While they are a work in progress—personally, relationally, and communally— their vision is clear: *to be a church for the West Valley.* In spite of, and often through their weaknesses, they long to move into the broken and beautiful culture around them with hope and joy and the transformative presence of Jesus Christ. They are a church with many young families, as well as students and seniors, where you expect a historic-yet-indigenous experience, much like the community of Emmaus! West Valley is a congregation of the Presbyterian Church in America.

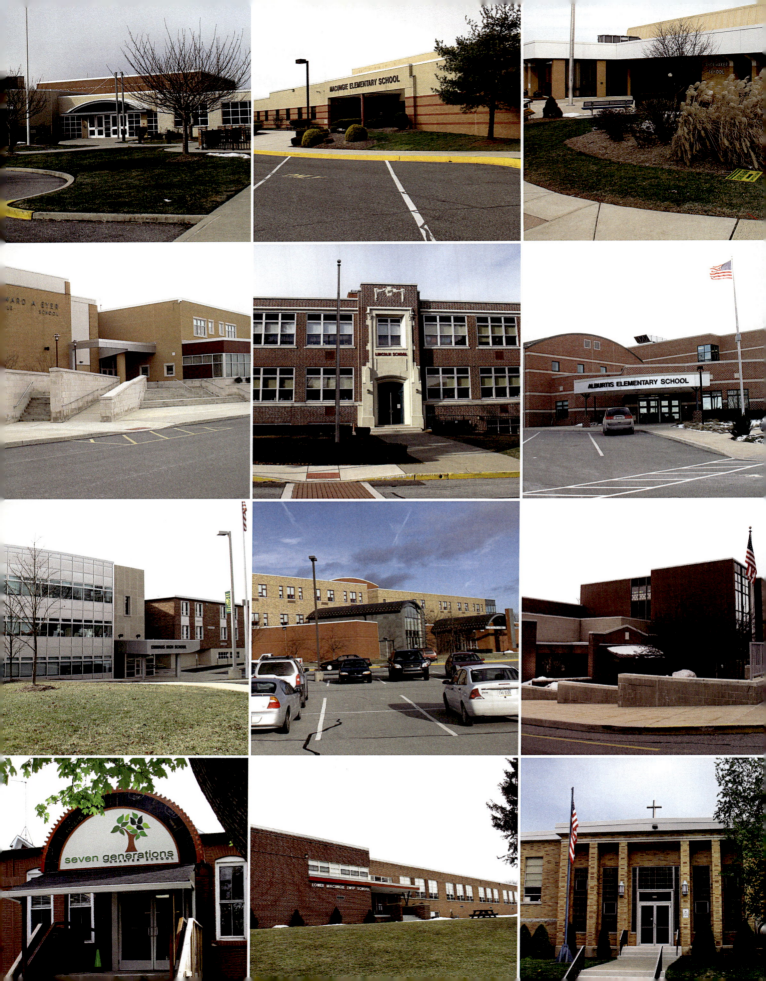

Emmaus Area Schools

The East Penn School District

Before Emmaus united with Macungie, Alburtis, Upper Milford Township, and Lower Macungie Township to form the East Penn School District in the 1950s, there were several schools located in Emmaus, including Central (1891), Washington (1910), Jefferson (1914), Lincoln (1928), and Thaddeus Stevens (1932). Each of the neighboring municipalities and townships also had their own schools and schools boards.

Following is the history of the East Penn School District Schools:

Alburtis Elementary School
222 W. Third Street
Alburtis, 18011
Date erected: 1957
New school built on site: 2004
Grade 1 to Grade 5

Jefferson Elementary School
520 Elm Street
Emmaus, 18049
Date erected: 1914
New school built on site: 1999
This was the site of Emmaus High School from 1914 to 1955 and then became the Jefferson Junior High School. The building was demolished and the new elementary school built on the site.
Kindergarten to Grade 5

Lincoln Elementary School
233 Seem Street
Emmaus, 18049
Date erected: 1928
Renovated: 1994
Kindergarten to Grade 5

Lower Macungie Elementary School
6043 Lower Macungie Road
Macungie, 18062
Date erected: 1951
This school was a Kindergarten to Grade 2 school. It c losed in 2005 and was re-opened as a Kindergarten Center in 2006.

Macungie Elementary School
4062 Brookside Road
Macungie, 18062
Date erected: 1989
Grade 1 to Grade 5

Shoemaker Elementary School
4068 Fairview Street
Macungie, 18062
Date erected: 1970
Grade 1 to Grade 5

Wescosville Elementary School
1064 Liberty Lane
Wescosville, 18106
Date erected: 1970
Renovated: 1997
In 1998-99 this school hosted Jefferson Elementary School students during Jefferson's construction.
Grade 1 to Grade 5

Lower Macungie Middle School
6299 Lower Macungie Road
Macungie, 18062
Date erected: 1998
Grade 6 to Grade 8

St. Ann's School
415 S. 6th St.
Emmaus, 18049
Classes started: 1949
School built: 1954
Kindergarten to Grade 8

Eyer Middle School
5616 Buckeye Road
Macungie, 18062
Date erected: 1973 as Junior High, 1998 as Middle School
Renovated: 2007
One-half day sessions were held for students of Lower Macungie Middle School in 1998 until LMMS's building construction was completed.
Grade 6 to Grade 8

Emmaus High School
500 Macungie Avenue
Emmaus, 18049
Date erected: 1954
Renovated: 1995-2000
Grade 9 to Grade 12

Seven Generations Charter School
154 Minor Street
Emmaus, 18049
Seven Generations Charter School is an environmental charter school in the East Penn School District that opened in September 2009 as a Kindergarten to 4th Grade school. In 2010, it offered Kindergarten to Grade 5.

Looking Back at History

SIGNIFICANT CHANGES HAVE TAKEN PLACE IN EMMAUS since the 200th anniversary celebration in 1959. Most notably, Emmaus continued to become more of a residential community. Over these years, advancing technologies enabled the establishment of smaller, nonmanufacturing and home-centered businesses. By 2009, there were 725 businesses in the Borough.

Meanwhile, the age profile, education status, and income distribution underwent important changes. At the same time, there was a perceptible increase in rentals in the Borough. These changes, in their totality, served to identify Emmaus as a true residential community whose citizens mainly worked elsewhere. Some of the major demographic statistics underwriting these changes are noted below:

By 2009, there were 11,924 residents (78 percent born in-state, 26 percent over age 60, and 24 percent under age 18). The median age of an Emmaus resident was 37.4 years. The top age groups were: 25–34 years of age—21 percent, 35–44 years of age—19 percent, and 45–54 years of age—17 percent. 22.1 percent were 65 or older. There were 47 percent males and 53 percent females living in town. There were 5,235 housing units, 68 percent owner occupied and 63 percent single family, of which 33 percent were built before 1939, and only 1.5 percent built since 2000.

Eighty-nine percent had a high school or higher education, with 31 percent having a bachelor degree or higher. 64.4 percent were married, 18.2 percent never married, 11.5 percent widowed, and 16.7 percent divorced. Median household income in 2008 dollars was $54,249, with an unemployment rate of 6.85 percent. Forty-nine percent of households had children under 18. The median value of an Emmaus home was $133,100.

These statistics clearly indicate that by 2009 Emmaus had become a residential bedroom community while, at the same time, becoming a magnet for small business development.

Since the 1959 Anniversary Celebration, Emmaus became the global headquarters for Rodale Inc., one of the world's largest publishers of health-related books and magazines. Buckeye Pipe Line, a US petroleum distributor, is also headquartered just outside of the Borough. Emmaus is also the home of Shangy's, one of the nation's largest beer distributors, featuring over 3,000 domestic and import beer brands, attracting thousands of beer enthusiasts from around the nation each year.

Yocco's Hot Dogs, known for its regionally famous hot dogs and cheese-steaks, has one of its six restaurants just west of Emmaus on Chestnut Street and maintains its corporate headquarters in Emmaus.

The largest major shopping mall in the Emmaus area is South Mall, located on Lehigh Street on Emmaus' border with Salisbury Township and Allentown.

Roger Whitcomb

{ 71

CIRCA 1920s

CIRCA 1980s

2010

SPILLA

72

CIRCA 1950s

Stately Spruce Tree, 'Born' in 1919 Storm, Downed by Recent Gale, Centers Emmaus Trim

A giant, bushy evergreen, whose life began and ended in the violence of a storm, is the Emmaus community Christmas tree which tonight begins radiating its seasonal cheer from the Triangle in the heart of the borough.

'Born' in Storm

"Born" of a storm at Penn State college in the summer of 1919, the stately arbor, a Norwegian spruce, died in the big blow of Nov. 25, 1950 after 31 years of domesticated life as an "orphan."

The tree, known to all Emmaus, was the property of Howard J. Yeager, superintendent of borough schools, who served as its guardian for more than two decades in memory of a close friend.

Yeager "willed the tree to the borough so the entire community may share in the beauty of its last stand on earth. It is being trimmed today by volunteers, and tonight at 6 it will be dedicated at a brief ceremony when its lights are turned on for the first time.

The tree's unusual story goes back to a session of summer school ... where the late Cal-... teacher, had

The Downtown Emmaus Triangle

THE BOROUGH OF EMMAUS is the only town in Pennsylvania with a triangle at its center. How this peculiar space came into being is an interesting story and deserves to be memorialized for future generations.

Martin J. Backenstoe was a general practitioner family doctor in Emmaus early in the twentieth century and served the community in numerous other ways, including Borough councilman and a director of a number of area banks. As a founder of the Emmaus National Bank, he served as president for fourteen years and then, as a founding partner of the Security Trust Company, he and some colleagues played a decisive role in the creation of the Emmaus Triangle Park.

The following commentary is taken from his autobiography, *Triumphant Living*, and is reprinted here with the permission of M. J. Backenstoe's grandson, Judge John E. Backenstoe:

"Wintering in Florida at the time [1909], the project (the creation of the Security Trust Company) was held up awaiting my return. Then a committee of seven esteemed friends called and prevailed on me to join and take an active part in the venture. The charter granted, organization completed, and being President, temporary quarters were secured facing the Triangle. Immediate success followed the opening of doors of the new bank in the Weaver Building at the Triangle.

The unsightly dilapidated Eagle Hotel, Livery Stable and wagon shed covered the Triangle grounds and preempted also considerable ground of the streets surrounding the Triangle. While still President of the Emmaus National and also Chairman of the Street Committee of Borough Council, I observed the traffic hazard surrounding the Triangle where was located the Eagle Hotel and horse structures. I advocated the tearing down of all the structures in the interest of the traveling public as well as beautifying the very heart of town. The proposition met with approval. Poverty was the convenient excuse. The temporary quarters occupied by the new bank soon became inadequate and we decided on a logical location for a permanent home and procured a firm option on the desired site, while not making public announcement thereof immediately. The selected location was ideal, providing the Hotel building was cleared before we erected the new building. But never would we build as long as the dilapidated Hotel eyesore remained and the street not widened to an adequate width, necessary for the safe and increasing traffic through the town's center—out Chestnut Street or up Main Street.

The problem was how to manage and accomplish the Triangle clearance, since the borough declined my second appeal for this improvement, claiming now the abutting property owners on the off sides of the Triangle were opposed to any changes in conditions and probabilities. I personally purchased the Triangle property for $18,000 and announced that as soon as possible a large bank building would occupy the Triangle site.

I was well aware that the Emmaus National Bank would leave no stone unturned to oppose the erection of such a building, standing as it would directly in front of their own building putting them thereby in the shade.

Promptly architectural designs were procured and a contract for the erection of a building on the Triangle was offered, and was almost to be signed when my telephone requested me to hold off the signing the contract. The Borough Solicitor, Richard W. Iobst, informed me that just then, the Borough had decided that all the Triangle structures were to be condemned, the site to be removed for a Public Park. Tentatively, we objected. Being in a fine strategic position, we finally succeeded in making a very favorable sale arrangement, transferring title to the Borough, but stipulated that no structure of any kind whatsoever, dare ever be erected on the plot. We accepted from the Borough a first mortgage on the property, and were pleased to have in our portfolio such a gilt-edge security, although for a small bank the loan was in excess of actual legal limits. The Borough then tore down all the buildings, widened the streets all around, and plotted an open triangular park on the site.

Dr. D.D. Fritch of Macungie said publicly, 'To the founder of the Security Trust Company is due the entire credit for this necessary civic improvement, in the heart of our town. Should there be a mishap to the two Emmaus Banks, the buildings will always stand as a monument to Dr. Backenstoe.' [Dr. H. T. Wicket and family then made a donation to the borough of the stone fountain pictured in the center of the Triangle as seen in the accompanying photo.]"

{ 73

EMMAUS COMMUNITY PARK

BOROUGH OF E

Fall 2005

Around Town
The Emmaus Borough News

Emmaus—On Top Again!!!

A Special Invitation From the Mayor

Celebration Weekend A Rousing Success

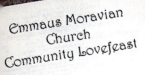

Emmaus Moravian
Church
Community Lovefeast

June 20, 2009

Preserving Our History

Emmaus Heritage Alliance

The Emmaus Heritage Alliance was formed in 1997 to foster cooperation among the groups already involved in promoting the heritage of Emmaus. This coalition—composed of the Emmaus Main Street Program, Shelter House Society, Knauss Homestead Preservation Society, the Friends of the 1803 House, the Emmaus Historical Society, Emmaus Moravian Church, God's Acre Cemetery, and the Emmaus Public Library—has worked together to "tell the story" of Emmaus. The groups have jointly planned events such as Heritage Days and Old Fashioned Christmas, with the goal of illustrating for the community the unique history of Emmaus.

In 2005, the Alliance launched a three-part historic signage project. The first phase of the project was the publishing of an informational brochure featuring the history of Emmaus and of each of the Alliance members. The second phase involved the design and installation of blue and white directional banners, guiding visitors to the various historic sites. The third and final phase was the design and installation of "interpretive" signs at the historic sites themselves to give visitors a brief description of 18th century life in Emmaus.

The Emmaus Heritage Alliance serves to coordinate the historic activities and events among its members. Behind the Alliance stands a wealth of knowledge, community involvement, a sincere interest in preserving Emmaus' rich history, and a strong desire to help educate all those who live, work and play in our community.

{ 75

Emmaus Public Library

The Emmaus Public Library owes its beginnings to the Emmaus High School Alumni Association, which accepted a bequest of the building at 348 Main Street from John D. Weaver in 1938. Until that building was ready for use as a library, the alumni association rented the first floor of 435 Chestnut Street. In 1944, the Main Street building opened, with a collection of 3,400 volumes.

By the mid-1960s, the collection had more than doubled and space became a problem. In 1965, Mayor Clarence Hoffert cast a tie-breaking vote in favor of a borough ordinance creating

the Emmaus Public Library. With federal and state funds and many contributions, the present building was opened on June 3, 1966. As years progressed, the collection grew to 48,000 volumes. An addition was planned, built, and opened in 1982.

In 1991, a generous donor provided the means to have the Margaret Knoll Gardner Lecture room added to the building. Now, in the 21st century, the library has grown to fill every square inch with books, CDs, and video material. A building campaign has started to raise funds for another addition, which will incorporate new space for children and a relaxed reading area for adults.

The Knauss Homestead

The Knauss family played a central role in the history of Emmaus. Along with Jacob Ehrenhardt, Sebastian Knauss donated a large tract of land for the congregational village that took shape in the mid-eighteenth century. The Knauss House is situated on part of the original two hundred acres and survives as one of the best-preserved 18th century buildings associated with the 1747 founding of the Moravian community of Emmaus. It was erected in 1777 by Heinrich Knauss, the eldest son of Sebastian, and is constructed of sawed (sawn) logs set into mortises within corner posts and, therefore, is considered a corner post plank house rather than a log home structure.

The house has undergone few significant alterations since its original construction and was inhabited for one hundred fifty eight consecutive years by descendants of Sebastian Knauss, with seven generations born within its walls.

The clapboard-sided house rises two and one-half stories above a pointed stone foundation and exists intact with most of the six-over-six sashes and trim, siding, and structure original to the house when it was constructed.

The interior is divided into four rooms on each floor, which are arranged around a central chimney. The main floor consists of a small hall providing access to the upper floors, the kitchen (*kuche*) and the main parlor (*stube*). The first floor bedroom (*kammer*) is accessible from both the kitchen and the parlor. There are four rooms on the second floor. Owned by the Borough, the Knauss Homestead is a work in progress.

Emmaus Main Street Program

By the early 1990s the central business district of Emmaus had been flanked by newly developed strip malls, which led to stiff competition from national retail chains, threatening the economic success of the downtown merchants. The Borough of Emmaus recognized that its traditional downtown, the heart of its community and commerce, was in danger of losing its viability and unique historical charm.

It formed the Emmaus Main Street Program (EMSP) in 1995 as a 5013C nonprofit organization with the purpose of preserving and revitalizing the historic downtown district of Emmaus. A board of directors formed to govern the EMSP.

The purpose of the Main Street Program is to stimulate economic development in Emmaus while preserving the borough's unique historic and cultural framework by attracting business to the historic downtown area, promoting the community, educating the immediate and surrounding area about Emmaus' exquisite quality of life, fostering community pride, offering cooperative advertising, coordinating and holding special events, improving the physical appearance of Emmaus, supporting preservation efforts, and encouraging cooperation and networking with other organizations.

The EMSP is a member-supported organization serving approximately seven hundred businesses and 12,000 residents of Emmaus. The program is associated with the National Main Street Center, Pennsylvania Downtown Center, which is the "voice of downtown revitalization in Pennsylvania."

Over the years, the EMSP has received from the State of Pennsylvania some $100,000 for a Streetscape Improvement Project, $100,000 for storefront façade enhancements, $20,000 to develop a Downtown Master Plan, as well as a $5,000 technology grant and $5,000 from Lehigh County for an Historical Signage Project.

The Emmaus Main Street Program continues to sponser community events, such as Emmaus Heritage Days and Old Fashioned Christmas, works closely with businesses to develop monthly promotions, serves as an advisor for new and startup businesses, serves on the East Penn Business Council Trails Project in the development of a five-borough-linked biking/walking trail, and serves with the Emmaus Heritage Alliance on a historic sites marker project.

{ **77**

1803 House

The story of the 1803 House, at 55 S. Keystone Avenue, began with German settlers who made their way north from the port of Philadelphia, following the Perkiomen Trail into the fertile valley that we know today as the Lehigh Valley. One settler was Jacob Ehrenhardt, a blacksmith and farmer from Marstadt, Germany, who arrived in Pennsylvania in 1739, and settled onto this land, which the Lenni Lenape called "machk-un-tschi," or "the feeding place of the bears." Eager for a place to worship, Jacob and his friend Sebastian Knauss visited the new Moravian community

of Bethlehem (est. 1741) and requested that the church provide their settlement with preachers. Over the next several years, they erected a log church, donated portions of their land for a new settlement, and persuaded the Bethlehem church to establish a "gemein-ort," or congregational village closed to all but "kindred spirits."

Jacob Ehrenhardt Jr. was born in 1760. Though raised to accept the strict limits imposed by the church, he risked censure by enlisting in the Northampton County Militia to fight in the American Revolution. Fortunately he joined a year before the end of the war, and he returned home safely and was accepted back into the Moravian congregation. Jacob and his wife, Susanna, had a family of four girls, and in 1803 built a Federal-style stone home on land he inherited from his father.

The house is typical of a German plan, which includes a kitchen (*kuche*), social room (*stube*), and parents' bedroom (*kammer*) on the ground floor. Upstairs consists of two bedrooms, an attic, and a smoking chamber over the kitchen area. What wasn't so typical was the home's impressive scale and its generous attention to detail. Jacob Jr.'s success in his occupations as shoemaker, farmer, and possibly a tavern keeper enabled him to create a structure that has remained surprisingly intact after withstanding more than two hundred years of hard use.

What was less certain was the fate of Jacob's homestead after his death in 1825. During the next one hundred fifty years the house would transfer ownership some ten times, be used as an apartment, and be left boarded up for demolition. Fortunately for Emmaus, the house was saved as a result of community spirit. In 1975, Robert and Ardath Rodale donated the house and its surrounding property to the borough, and soon after a committee was assembled to oversee the restoration.

The Friends of the 1803 House, Inc., a nonprofit organization, was formed in 1977, with the mission of preserving the homestead and promoting an appreciation for local history. Through the hard work of volunteers, local citizens, and businesses, what was once a house in need of major repair is now restored, furnished to the period, and open to the public as a museum. The 1803 House is listed in the National Register of Historic Places, and today it is available for the enjoyment of the community, as well as for educational programs. Through student, group and individual tours, one can walk through the door to Jacob's home and enter into the early 19th century beginnings of Emmaus.

Emmaus Moravian Church

In contrast to most other Moravian settlements, Emmaus became a Moravian community by default rather than by design. By the 1730s there were already numerous German-speaking settlers, largely of the Reformed Lutheran faiths. There was much dissension here as elsewhere concerning the new-felt sense of individual freedom and the lack of clergy, which resulted in the lack of proper leadership. With the coming of the Moravians to Bethlehem in 1742, it soon became apparent that ministering to the unchurched German settlers was as important as reaching out to the Indians. Consequently, many ministers were sent out to the hinterlands to help the needy, usually after a request by the settlers themselves.

This situation also applied to the Emmaus area. Two men, Sebastian Knauss and Jacob Ehrenhardt were distressed by the need for trained ministers. For that reason, they appealed to Bethlehem for assistance. This proved successful, to the point that Brethren Knauss, Ehrenhardt, and several others set up a Moravian Fellowship here on July 30, 1747. The Emmaus Moravian Church grew out of what they formally organized at that time.

Originally Emmaus was known by its Indian name, "Maguntsche" (machk-un-tschi). There was no town yet, only an area. Later on when the area was organized into townships, it was given the name "Salzburg" (Salisbury today). It was not until 1761 that Bishop Spangenberg officially named the town "Emmaus." From its beginning in 1747 to 1838, Emmaus was a closed community. Only those who were members of the Emmaus Moravian Congregation could live here. By the mid 1800s this system became untenable and the closed community was opened up to all faiths.

The Shelter House

The Shelter House (*Zufluchtshaus*, a house of shelter) is a two-story, eight-room Germanic log structure located on the northern slope of South Mountain beyond the end of 4th Street on the southern edge of Emmaus. Listed in the National Registry of Historic Places (built by early settlers around 1734), the Shelter House is believed to be the oldest continually inhabited dwelling in the Lehigh Valley.

{ 79

Recently, the Shelter House was featured as the flagship log house for the Lehigh Log Cabin Trail Project. Board members and members at large of the Shelter House Society maintain the historic log structure, opening it to the public by appointment and during annual festivals. Soon, the Shelter House Society will launch a project to restore a stone and wooden springhouse on the property. Resident curator Dean Bortz offers private tours and serves as the architectural and historical authority on the Shelter House.

Emmaus Historical Society

The Emmaus Historical Society was formed in February 1992 at the urging of Mayor Robert Bastian and Patricia Shirock, chairwoman of the Parks and Recreation Committee of the Emmaus Borough Council. The organization was incorporated in April 1993 through the effort of John Corbett and the cooperation of State Representative Don Snyder. The goals of the Society as enumerated in its charter are to preserve the social history of Emmaus through research and study of its industry, educational system, religious heritage, genealogy, hotels and

inns, businesses, agriculture, and municipal agreements, while obtaining artifacts and photographs of these areas of interest. In addition, the Society makes items available for research and education, preserves Emmaus memorabilia, and obtains written history through interviews and articles.

In February 1999, the Society acquired the property at 563 Chestnut Street and after extensive remodeling, opened the building as a museum in December of that year. In 2007, after five years of research, the organization published a beautifully bound and illustrated book in honor of the men and women from Emmaus who served in World War II.

More recently, in cooperation with Scott Stoneback of the Media People, the Society produced a DVD containing interviews of fifty-eight borough residents. On Memorial Day 2009, the organization dedicated a marker at the Memorial Triangle engraved with the names of the thirty-nine men and one woman from Emmaus who died in wars dating from the Civil War to Iraq. At the present time the Society has grown to a membership of more than six hundred. The Society also serves as the Visitors' Center for Emmaus.

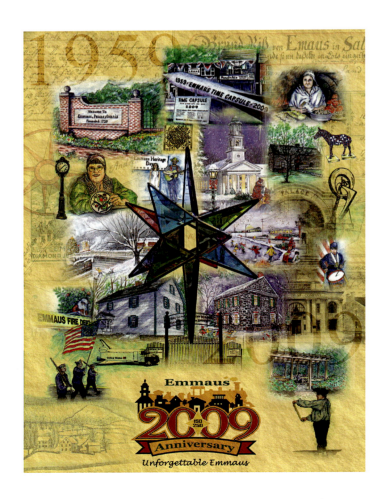

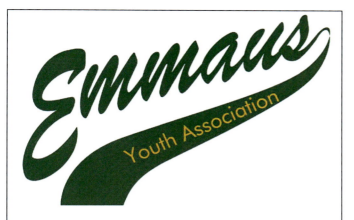

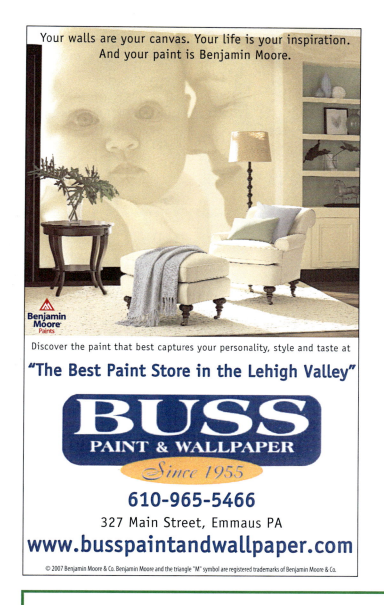
A BIG Thank You!

The members of the 2009 Anniversary Steering Committee wish to thank all those individuals and organizations that helped to make the commemoration a success. We greatly appreciate all those who gave generously of their talents and time to contribute to this wonderful year. The friendships made and strengthened will remain in our hearts for many years to come.

Sincerely,

Alison, Audrey, Corrine, Craig, Dave, Diane, Gene, George,
Johanna, John, Karen, Kathy, Lee Ann, Marge, Martha, Mike,
Nate, Richard, Roger, Ruth, Sam, Steve, Teri S-M, and Teri M.